This journal belongs to

_____

START DATE _____   END DATE _____

If found, please return to

_____

Nourishment

A FIVE-YEAR JOURNAL
of TASTE MEMORIES

How to Use this Book

If it seems like your life revolves around food, well, that's probably because it does! This journal provides a framework for recording your day-to-day mealtime choices, and tracking the impact and evolution of those choices. Each day, jot down a few thoughts about food—what you ate that day and how you felt: positive, negative, hungry, happy, harried. Maybe you are working toward a specific goal: trying new recipes, eating out less, eating out more, shopping local . . . this is the place to track your progress! Use the provided scale to record how nourished you feel—physically, mentally, emotionally—at the end of each day.

As the journal is filled, look back at the good days and relive those delicious taste memories—and learn from the not-so-good days how to make everyday mealtime choices work for **you**.

———————◆———————

"I was born hungry."
—JULIA CHILD

JANUARY
4

20 18 | First day of trying to cut out sugar... yikes. I did have a great convo with my barista this morning about habits-making and breaking them. Takeaway: this is going to be harder than I thought.

① ② ● ④ ⑤

20 19 | Can't believe I was trying to cut out sugar a year ago—that seems like another life. This morning I had a homemade cinnamon roll for breakfast and have never felt better. I need to remember to save that recipe.

① ② ③ ④ ●

1

"The world begins at a kitchen table."

—JOY HARJO, "PERHAPS THE WORLD ENDS HERE"

20 _____
① ② ③ ④ ⑤

20 _____
① ② ③ ④ ⑤

20 _____
① ② ③ ④ ⑤

20 _____
① ② ③ ④ ⑤

20 _____
① ② ③ ④ ⑤

"Progress in civilization has been accompanied by progress in cookery."

—FANNIE FARMER

20

① ② ③ ④ ⑤

20

① ② ③ ④ ⑤

20

① ② ③ ④ ⑤

20

① ② ③ ④ ⑤

20

① ② ③ ④ ⑤

*"Breakfast is everything. The beginning, the first thing.
It is the mouthful that is the commitment to the new day."*

—A.A. GILL

20

1
2
3
4
5

20

1
2
3
4
5

20

1
2
3
4
5

20

1
2
3
4
5

20

1
2
3
4
5

"I was born hungry."
—JULIA CHILD

20 ___

①
②
③
④
⑤

20 ___

①
②
③
④
⑤

20 ___

①
②
③
④
⑤

20 ___

①
②
③
④
⑤

20 ___

①
②
③
④
⑤

5

*"Tell me what kind of food you eat,
and I will tell you what kind of man you are."*

—JEAN ANTHELME BRILLAT-SAVARIN

20

① ② ③ ④ ⑤

20

① ② ③ ④ ⑤

20

① ② ③ ④ ⑤

20

① ② ③ ④ ⑤

20

① ② ③ ④ ⑤

"Devote all the time and resources at your disposal to the building up of a fine kitchen."

—ELIZABETH DAVID

20___

① ② ③ ④ ⑤

20___

① ② ③ ④ ⑤

20___

① ② ③ ④ ⑤

20___

① ② ③ ④ ⑤

20___

① ② ③ ④ ⑤

"*Cooking is an essential human activity.*"

—MARK BITTMAN

20 _____

①
②
③
④
⑤

20 _____

①
②
③
④
⑤

20 _____

①
②
③
④
⑤

20 _____

①
②
③
④
⑤

20 _____

①
②
③
④
⑤

*"After a good dinner one can forgive
anybody, even one's own relations."*

—OSCAR WILDE, *A WOMAN OF NO IMPORTANCE*

20

① ② ③ ④ ⑤

20

① ② ③ ④ ⑤

20

① ② ③ ④ ⑤

20

① ② ③ ④ ⑤

20

① ② ③ ④ ⑤

9

"You can't just eat food," he said. "You've got to talk about it, too."

—KURT VONNEGUT, *JAILBIRD*

20 ⌐

① ② ③ ④ ⑤

20 ⌐

① ② ③ ④ ⑤

20 ⌐

① ② ③ ④ ⑤

20 ⌐

① ② ③ ④ ⑤

20 ⌐

① ② ③ ④ ⑤

20 _____

①
②
③
④
⑤

20 _____

①
②
③
④
⑤

20 _____

①
②
③
④
⑤

20 _____

①
②
③
④
⑤

20 _____

①
②
③
④
⑤

11

*"Food served is always more than just food served.
That is to say, it is more than just fuel for the body."*

—MAYA ANGELOU

20 _____

① ____
② ____
③ ____
④ ____
⑤ ____

20 _____

① ____
② ____
③ ____
④ ____
⑤ ____

20 _____

① ____
② ____
③ ____
④ ____
⑤ ____

20 _____

① ____
② ____
③ ____
④ ____
⑤ ____

20 _____

① ____
② ____
③ ____
④ ____
⑤ ____

"There are endless ways to think about food."

—ALICE WATERS

20 [ ]

①
②
③
④
⑤

20 [ ]

①
②
③
④
⑤

20 [ ]

①
②
③
④
⑤

20 [ ]

①
②
③
④
⑤

20 [ ]

①
②
③
④
⑤

*"Food is a necessary component to life.
People can live without Renoir, Mozart, Gaudí,
Beckett, but they cannot live without food."*
—GRANT ACHATZ

20 _____ ① ② ③ ④ ⑤

20 _____ ① ② ③ ④ ⑤

20 _____ ① ② ③ ④ ⑤

20 _____ ① ② ③ ④ ⑤

20 _____ ① ② ③ ④ ⑤

"'Tis an ill cook that cannot lick his own fingers."
—WILLIAM SHAKESPEARE, *ROMEO AND JULIET*

20

①
②
③
④
⑤

20

①
②
③
④
⑤

20

①
②
③
④
⑤

20

①
②
③
④
⑤

20

①
②
③
④
⑤

"There can be no more shameful carelessness than with the food we eat for life itself. When we exist without thought or thanksgiving we are not men, but beasts."

—M.F.K. FISHER

20

① ② ③ ④ ⑤

20

① ② ③ ④ ⑤

20

① ② ③ ④ ⑤

20

① ② ③ ④ ⑤

20

① ② ③ ④ ⑤

"*The idea is to eat well and not die from it—for the simple reason that that would be the end of your eating.*"

—JIM HARRISON

20

① ② ③ ④ ⑤

20

① ② ③ ④ ⑤

20

① ② ③ ④ ⑤

20

① ② ③ ④ ⑤

20

① ② ③ ④ ⑤

17

"When you eat well, you are eating memory."
—BARRY HANNAH, *YONDER STANDS YOUR ORPHAN*

20 ____

① ② ③ ④ ⑤

20 ____

① ② ③ ④ ⑤

20 ____

① ② ③ ④ ⑤

20 ____

① ② ③ ④ ⑤

20 ____

① ② ③ ④ ⑤

"I want my meals to last forever."

—NORA EPHRON

20 ⌐

① ② ③ ④ ⑤

20 ⌐

① ② ③ ④ ⑤

20 ⌐

① ② ③ ④ ⑤

20 ⌐

① ② ③ ④ ⑤

20 ⌐

① ② ③ ④ ⑤

JANUARY
19

"Most of life's problems can be solved with a good cookie."

—INA GARTEN

20 _____

①
②
③
④
⑤

20 _____

①
②
③
④
⑤

20 _____

①
②
③
④
⑤

20 _____

①
②
③
④
⑤

20 _____

①
②
③
④
⑤

"Nothing would be more tiresome than eating and drinking if God had not made them a pleasure as well as a necessity."

—VOLTAIRE

20

① ② ③ ④ ⑤

20

① ② ③ ④ ⑤

20

① ② ③ ④ ⑤

20

① ② ③ ④ ⑤

20

① ② ③ ④ ⑤

*"Do not be afraid to talk about food.
Food which is worth eating is worth discussing."*

—X. MARCEL BOULESTIN

20 _____
_____
_____
_____
_____

① ② ③ ④ ⑤

20 _____
_____
_____
_____
_____

① ② ③ ④ ⑤

20 _____
_____
_____
_____
_____

① ② ③ ④ ⑤

20 _____
_____
_____
_____
_____

① ② ③ ④ ⑤

20 _____
_____
_____
_____
_____

① ② ③ ④ ⑤

> *"I mind my belly very studiously, and very carefully;*
> *for I look upon it, that he who does not mind*
> *his belly will hardly mind anything else."*
>
> —SAMUEL JOHNSON

20 _____

① _____
② _____
③ _____
④ _____
⑤ _____

20 _____

① _____
② _____
③ _____
④ _____
⑤ _____

20 _____

① _____
② _____
③ _____
④ _____
⑤ _____

20 _____

① _____
② _____
③ _____
④ _____
⑤ _____

20 _____

① _____
② _____
③ _____
④ _____
⑤ _____

"That's something I've noticed about food: whenever there's a crisis if you can get people to eating normally things get better."

—MADELEINE L'ENGLE, *THE MOON BY NIGHT*

20

①
②
③
④
⑤

20

①
②
③
④
⑤

20

①
②
③
④
⑤

20

①
②
③
④
⑤

20

①
②
③
④
⑤

"Eating is one of the most important aspects of living. I like indulging. I like to eat one food at a time, to savour each individual thing."

—MARCO PIERRE WHITE

20

① ② ③ ④ ⑤

20

① ② ③ ④ ⑤

20

① ② ③ ④ ⑤

20

① ② ③ ④ ⑤

20

① ② ③ ④ ⑤

JANUARY
25

*"Great sorrow or great joy should bring intense hunger—
not abstinence from food, as our novelists will have it."*
—SIR ARTHUR CONAN DOYLE, *THE POISON BELT*

20

① ② ③ ④ ⑤

20

① ② ③ ④ ⑤

20

① ② ③ ④ ⑤

20

① ② ③ ④ ⑤

20

① ② ③ ④ ⑤

"People who have tried it, tell me that a clear conscience makes you very happy and contented; but a full stomach does the business quite as well, and is cheaper, and more easily obtained."

—JEROME K. JEROME, *THREE MEN IN A BOAT*

JANUARY
26

20 ⎤
          ① ② ③ ④ ⑤

20 ⎤
          ① ② ③ ④ ⑤

20 ⎤
          ① ② ③ ④ ⑤

20 ⎤
          ① ② ③ ④ ⑤

20 ⎤
          ① ② ③ ④ ⑤

27

"The proper study of mankind . . . ? Food?"

—SYBILLE BEDFORD, *JIGSAW: AN UNSENTIMENTAL EDUCATION*

20 _____

① ② ③ ④ ⑤

20 _____

① ② ③ ④ ⑤

20 _____

① ② ③ ④ ⑤

20 _____

① ② ③ ④ ⑤

20 _____

① ② ③ ④ ⑤

"I have made a lot of mistakes falling in love, and regretted most of them, but never the potatoes that went with them."

—NORA EPHRON

20

① ② ③ ④ ⑤

20

① ② ③ ④ ⑤

20

① ② ③ ④ ⑤

20

① ② ③ ④ ⑤

20

① ② ③ ④ ⑤

"Whatever happens in a house, robbery or murder, it doesn't matter, you must have your breakfast."

—WILKIE COLLINS, *THE MOONSTONE*

20

① ② ③ ④ ⑤

20

① ② ③ ④ ⑤

20

① ② ③ ④ ⑤

20

① ② ③ ④ ⑤

20

① ② ③ ④ ⑤

"Although it's possible to love eating without being able to cook, I don't believe you can ever really cook unless you love eating."

—NIGELLA LAWSON

JANUARY
30

20 _____

① ② ③ ④ ⑤

20 _____

① ② ③ ④ ⑤

20 _____

① ② ③ ④ ⑤

20 _____

① ② ③ ④ ⑤

20 _____

① ② ③ ④ ⑤

"Salt is the difference between eating in Technicolor and eating in black and white."
—JAY RAYNER

20

① ② ③ ④ ⑤

20

① ② ③ ④ ⑤

20

① ② ③ ④ ⑤

20

① ② ③ ④ ⑤

20

① ② ③ ④ ⑤

"Deliciousness is the final criterion."

—DORIE GREENSPAN

20 ___

① ② ③ ④ ⑤

20 ___

① ② ③ ④ ⑤

20 ___

① ② ③ ④ ⑤

20 ___

① ② ③ ④ ⑤

20 ___

① ② ③ ④ ⑤

2

"If you do anything perfectly, even something as simple as a hamburger, it's everlasting."

—JEREMIAH TOWER

20

① ② ③ ④ ⑤

20

① ② ③ ④ ⑤

20

① ② ③ ④ ⑤

20

① ② ③ ④ ⑤

20

① ② ③ ④ ⑤

"Why would anybody ever eat anything besides breakfast food?"
—LESLIE KNOPE, *PARKS AND RECREATION*

20

①
②
③
④
⑤

20

①
②
③
④
⑤

20

①
②
③
④
⑤

20

①
②
③
④
⑤

20

①
②
③
④
⑤

4

"Cooking is a field in which familiarity does not breed contempt."

—CRAIG CLAIBORNE

20

① ② ③ ④ ⑤

20

① ② ③ ④ ⑤

20

① ② ③ ④ ⑤

20

① ② ③ ④ ⑤

20

① ② ③ ④ ⑤

"The history of cooking is in many ways like the history of language, or the history of folk music—a matter of borrowing, adapting, evolving."

—MARTHA STEWART

20

①
②
③
④
⑤

20

①
②
③
④
⑤

20

①
②
③
④
⑤

20

①
②
③
④
⑤

20

①
②
③
④
⑤

"Cakes are healthy too, you just eat a thin slice."

—MARY BERRY

20 _____

① _____
② _____
③ _____
④ _____
⑤ _____

20 _____

① _____
② _____
③ _____
④ _____
⑤ _____

20 _____

① _____
② _____
③ _____
④ _____
⑤ _____

20 _____

① _____
② _____
③ _____
④ _____
⑤ _____

20 _____

① _____
② _____
③ _____
④ _____
⑤ _____

"A great dish hits you like a Whip-It: There's momentary elation, a brief ripple of pure pleasure in the spacetime continuum."

—DAVID CHANG

20

① ② ③ ④ ⑤

20

① ② ③ ④ ⑤

20

① ② ③ ④ ⑤

20

① ② ③ ④ ⑤

20

① ② ③ ④ ⑤

FEBRUARY

8

"[T]his is what gets me excited—the multitude of ingredients cooked and processed by so many people in so many ways with so many different purposes."

—YOTAM OTTOLENGHI

20

① ② ③ ④ ⑤

20

① ② ③ ④ ⑤

20

① ② ③ ④ ⑤

20

① ② ③ ④ ⑤

20

① ② ③ ④ ⑤

"It was quicker for my dad to find a wife than it is for me to decide where to eat dinner."

—AZIZ ANSARI

20

① ② ③ ④ ⑤

20

① ② ③ ④ ⑤

20

① ② ③ ④ ⑤

20

① ② ③ ④ ⑤

20

① ② ③ ④ ⑤

"Cooking is like a dialogue between the chef and the people eating the food, and you need to be able to converse back-and-forth."

—RICK BAYLESS

20____

① ② ③ ④ ⑤

20____

① ② ③ ④ ⑤

20____

① ② ③ ④ ⑤

20____

① ② ③ ④ ⑤

20____

① ② ③ ④ ⑤

"The way food makes me feel is the one relationship I've never doubted."

—ASHLEY CHRISTENSEN

20 _____

① _____
② _____
③ _____
④ _____
⑤ _____

20 _____

① _____
② _____
③ _____
④ _____
⑤ _____

20 _____

① _____
② _____
③ _____
④ _____
⑤ _____

20 _____

① _____
② _____
③ _____
④ _____
⑤ _____

20 _____

① _____
② _____
③ _____
④ _____
⑤ _____

FEBRUARY

12

*"When you cook, you can accomplish something.
You can eat and also feed someone, be part of
something and bring people together."*

—DANNY BOWIEN

20

① ② ③ ④ ⑤

20

① ② ③ ④ ⑤

20

① ② ③ ④ ⑤

20

① ② ③ ④ ⑤

20

① ② ③ ④ ⑤

"Although Eating Honey was a very good thing to do, there was a moment just before you began to eat it which was better than when you were, but he didn't know what it was called."

—A.A. MILNE, *THE HOUSE AT POOH CORNER*

FEBRUARY
13

20

① ② ③ ④ ⑤

20

① ② ③ ④ ⑤

20

① ② ③ ④ ⑤

20

① ② ③ ④ ⑤

20

① ② ③ ④ ⑤

*"Food can be magic. It is magic. And yet it's not.
It comes from somewhere—and from someplace
and someone. Always. Food tells a story."*

—ANTHONY BOURDAIN

20 _____

① ② ③ ④ ⑤

20 _____

① ② ③ ④ ⑤

20 _____

① ② ③ ④ ⑤

20 _____

① ② ③ ④ ⑤

20 _____

① ② ③ ④ ⑤

"Who wants to live in a mansion if you have to subsist on vegetables and chaff?"

—MO YAN, *POW!*

20

①
②
③
④
⑤

20

①
②
③
④
⑤

20

①
②
③
④
⑤

20

①
②
③
④
⑤

20

①
②
③
④
⑤

FEBRUARY

16

"Then, of course, there is the moment when that warm bread comes from the oven and the aroma envelops you; you just have to sit down with a big slab of fresh bread and butter and a glass of wine."

—JAMES BEARD

20

①
②
③
④
⑤

20

①
②
③
④
⑤

20

①
②
③
④
⑤

20

①
②
③
④
⑤

20

①
②
③
④
⑤

"I'm constantly asked, 'What's the most important tool in the kitchen?' For me, it's hands. They give us the authority to call any dish ours."

—MARCUS SAMUELSSON

20 ⎡
_____
① _____
_____
② _____
_____
③ _____
_____
④ _____
_____
⑤ _____

20 ⎡
_____
① _____
_____
② _____
_____
③ _____
_____
④ _____
_____
⑤ _____

20 ⎡
_____
① _____
_____
② _____
_____
③ _____
_____
④ _____
_____
⑤ _____

20 ⎡
_____
① _____
_____
② _____
_____
③ _____
_____
④ _____
_____
⑤ _____

20 ⎡
_____
① _____
_____
② _____
_____
③ _____
_____
④ _____
_____
⑤ _____

18

"The best thing you can do for someone is make them a beautiful plate of food. How else can you invade someone's body without actually touching them?"

—PADMA LAKSHMI

20 _____
_____
_____
_____
_____

① ② ③ ④ ⑤

20 _____
_____
_____
_____
_____

① ② ③ ④ ⑤

20 _____
_____
_____
_____
_____

① ② ③ ④ ⑤

20 _____
_____
_____
_____
_____

① ② ③ ④ ⑤

20 _____
_____
_____
_____
_____

① ② ③ ④ ⑤

"Like in music, it's very important to have a balanced style when you eat. Meat makes people more aggressive; vegetables make you more relaxed."

—LANG LANG

20

① ② ③ ④ ⑤

20

① ② ③ ④ ⑤

20

① ② ③ ④ ⑤

20

① ② ③ ④ ⑤

20

① ② ③ ④ ⑤

"The object in teaching cookery is not to increase or complicate the work, not to make it a ceremonial, but to point out the simple and easy way."

—SARAH TYSON RORER

20 _____
_____
① ② ③ ④ ⑤

20 _____
_____
① ② ③ ④ ⑤

20 _____
_____
① ② ③ ④ ⑤

20 _____
_____
① ② ③ ④ ⑤

20 _____
_____
① ② ③ ④ ⑤

"The dish in the middle of the table is like the song you put on for everyone to start grooving to."

—ACTION BRONSON

FEBRUARY
21

20

①
②
③
④
⑤

20

①
②
③
④
⑤

20

①
②
③
④
⑤

20

①
②
③
④
⑤

20

①
②
③
④
⑤

"In cooking, care is half the battle."
—AUGUSTE ESCOFFIER

20

① ② ③ ④ ⑤

20

① ② ③ ④ ⑤

20

① ② ③ ④ ⑤

20

① ② ③ ④ ⑤

20

① ② ③ ④ ⑤

"It is a mistake to think that expensive food
necessarily means a good dinner."

—RUTH LOWINSKY

20

① ② ③ ④ ⑤

20

① ② ③ ④ ⑤

20

① ② ③ ④ ⑤

20

① ② ③ ④ ⑤

20

① ② ③ ④ ⑤

"I am a shoveller, a quantity man, and I
like to keep going until I feel sick."

—DAVID SEDARIS

20

① ② ③ ④ ⑤

20

① ② ③ ④ ⑤

20

① ② ③ ④ ⑤

20

① ② ③ ④ ⑤

20

① ② ③ ④ ⑤

"You learn a lot about someone when you share a meal together."
—ANTHONY BOURDAIN

20

①
②
③
④
⑤

20

①
②
③
④
⑤

20

①
②
③
④
⑤

20

①
②
③
④
⑤

20

①
②
③
④
⑤

FEBRUARY 26

"I am honored when someone asks me to help in the kitchen. That's when I know they're really letting me into their life."

—GIADA DE LAURENTIIS

20

① ② ③ ④ ⑤

20

① ② ③ ④ ⑤

20

① ② ③ ④ ⑤

20

① ② ③ ④ ⑤

20

① ② ③ ④ ⑤

"When you pay attention, cooking becomes a kind of meditation."

—RUTH REICHL

20

①
②
③
④
⑤

20

①
②
③
④
⑤

20

①
②
③
④
⑤

20

①
②
③
④
⑤

20

①
②
③
④
⑤

"It's all about getting the best ingredients. If you're the best chef in the world and you buy old fish, it's going to be smelly and nobody will like it."

—WOLFGANG PUCK

20

① ② ③ ④ ⑤

20

① ② ③ ④ ⑤

20

① ② ③ ④ ⑤

20

① ② ③ ④ ⑤

20

① ② ③ ④ ⑤

> *"If you really want to make a friend, go to someone's house and eat with him. . . . The people who give you their food give you their heart."*
> —CESAR CHAVEZ

20 ___

①
②
③
④
⑤

20 ___

①
②
③
④
⑤

20 ___

①
②
③
④
⑤

20 ___

①
②
③
④
⑤

20 ___

①
②
③
④
⑤

"A sameness in food (no matter how good it may be) palls upon the appetite."

—MARIA PARLOA

20 _____

① ②
③
④
⑤

20 _____

① ②
③
④
⑤

20 _____

① ②
③
④
⑤

20 _____

① ②
③
④
⑤

20 _____

① ②
③
④
⑤

> *"I think food is language—just like any other language it has a system, it has a structure, it has references it draws from and it has values."*
>
> —EDDIE HUANG

20

① ② ③ ④ ⑤

20

① ② ③ ④ ⑤

20

① ② ③ ④ ⑤

20

① ② ③ ④ ⑤

20

① ② ③ ④ ⑤

"I don't eat for memory. I eat because I love what I'm going to eat, and then it brings the memory."

—ERIC RIPERT

20

① ② ③ ④ ⑤

20

① ② ③ ④ ⑤

20

① ② ③ ④ ⑤

20

① ② ③ ④ ⑤

20

① ② ③ ④ ⑤

"*Great food happens at the intersection of your ingredients and your imagination.*"

—DANIEL PATTERSON

20 ⬚

①
②
③
④
⑤

20 ⬚

①
②
③
④
⑤

20 ⬚

①
②
③
④
⑤

20 ⬚

①
②
③
④
⑤

20 ⬚

①
②
③
④
⑤

"Seeking just the right preparation to magnify the charms of a knobby potato, skinny stalk of asparagus, or the first freshly shelled walnuts of the year is always a happy challenge."

—JUDY RODGERS

20

① ② ③ ④ ⑤

20

① ② ③ ④ ⑤

20

① ② ③ ④ ⑤

20

① ② ③ ④ ⑤

20

① ② ③ ④ ⑤

"Color is flavor!"

—NANCY SILVERTON

MARCH
6

20

① ② ③ ④ ⑤

20

① ② ③ ④ ⑤

20

① ② ③ ④ ⑤

20

① ② ③ ④ ⑤

20

① ② ③ ④ ⑤

"*I fear that people have lost a common-sense ability to decide for themselves—sometimes I'm not even sure they know what they want to eat.*"

—GABRIELLE HAMILTON

20 _____

① ② ③ ④ ⑤

20 _____

① ② ③ ④ ⑤

20 _____

① ② ③ ④ ⑤

20 _____

① ② ③ ④ ⑤

20 _____

① ② ③ ④ ⑤

> "The only way to become a cook is to cook, and the road to becoming a good cook is paved not only with repetition but also with the intuition you gain along the way."
>
> —JULIA TURSHEN

20

① ② ③ ④ ⑤

20

① ② ③ ④ ⑤

20

① ② ③ ④ ⑤

20

① ② ③ ④ ⑤

20

① ② ③ ④ ⑤

*"That's the way Chinese mothers show they love their
children, not through hugs and kisses but with stern
offerings of steamed dumplings, duck's gizzards, and crab."*

—AMY TAN, *THE JOY LUCK CLUB*

20 _____

① ② ③ ④ ⑤

20 _____

① ② ③ ④ ⑤

20 _____

① ② ③ ④ ⑤

20 _____

① ② ③ ④ ⑤

20 _____

① ② ③ ④ ⑤

"Good cooks are always at their best when they are not overthinking what they're doing—but instead making their particular specialties."

—BOBBY FLAY

20

①
②
③
④
⑤

20

①
②
③
④
⑤

20

①
②
③
④
⑤

20

①
②
③
④
⑤

20

①
②
③
④
⑤

"Food is imbued with cultural intimacy, defined by the unique nature of local ingredients, and experienced by different societies in a thousand unique ways."

—CHRISTOPHER KIMBALL

20 ___

① ② ③ ④ ⑤

20 ___

① ② ③ ④ ⑤

20 ___

① ② ③ ④ ⑤

20 ___

① ② ③ ④ ⑤

20 ___

① ② ③ ④ ⑤

"I always thought 'That's the way the cookie crumbles' is sort of demeaning to cookies. They don't crumble. They maybe break up, but then you've just got lots of little cookie pieces around."

—WALLY "FAMOUS" AMOS

MARCH

12

20

① ② ③ ④ ⑤

20

① ② ③ ④ ⑤

20

① ② ③ ④ ⑤

20

① ② ③ ④ ⑤

20

① ② ③ ④ ⑤

"If I'm going to die of anything, it's going to be gluttony."

—JUSTIN TIMBERLAKE

20

① ② ③ ④ ⑤

20

① ② ③ ④ ⑤

20

① ② ③ ④ ⑤

20

① ② ③ ④ ⑤

20

① ② ③ ④ ⑤

"Gathering at the table for breakfast allows us to weave our lives with others—and that should be a daily pleasure."

—MARION CUNNINGHAM

20 ___

① ___
② ___
③ ___
④ ___
⑤ ___

20 ___

① ___
② ___
③ ___
④ ___
⑤ ___

20 ___

① ___
② ___
③ ___
④ ___
⑤ ___

20 ___

① ___
② ___
③ ___
④ ___
⑤ ___

20 ___

① ___
② ___
③ ___
④ ___
⑤ ___

"The best poet is he who prepares our daily bread: the nearest baker who does not imagine himself to be a god."

—PABLO NERUDA

20 ⌐

① ② ③ ④ ⑤

20 ⌐

① ② ③ ④ ⑤

20 ⌐

① ② ③ ④ ⑤

20 ⌐

① ② ③ ④ ⑤

20 ⌐

① ② ③ ④ ⑤

"Hamburgers! The cornerstone of any nutritious breakfast."
—JULES, *PULP FICTION*

20 _____

①
②
③
④
⑤

20 _____

①
②
③
④
⑤

20 _____

①
②
③
④
⑤

20 _____

①
②
③
④
⑤

20 _____

①
②
③
④
⑤

"The glutton demands quantity, the epicure quality."

—ALEXANDRE DUMAS

20 |
① ② ③ ④ ⑤

20 |
① ② ③ ④ ⑤

20 |
① ② ③ ④ ⑤

20 |
① ② ③ ④ ⑤

20 |
① ② ③ ④ ⑤

"Food is the easiest way to bridge gaps, build friendships, and become family . . . All in one day."

—ANDREW ZIMMERN

MARCH

18

20 ⌐

① ② ③ ④ ⑤

20 ⌐

① ② ③ ④ ⑤

20 ⌐

① ② ③ ④ ⑤

20 ⌐

① ② ③ ④ ⑤

20 ⌐

① ② ③ ④ ⑤

MARCH

19

*"I think bread is the perfect mythic symbol
to explain the meaning of life."*

—PETER REINHART

20

① ② ③ ④ ⑤

20

① ② ③ ④ ⑤

20

① ② ③ ④ ⑤

20

① ② ③ ④ ⑤

20

① ② ③ ④ ⑤

"*Perfection [in cooking] is rare because it is all tied up with you and the elements, in an unfathomable alchemy that the slightest change in moisture, wind, or phase of the moon can upset.*"

—DIANA KENNEDY

20

① ② ③ ④ ⑤

20

① ② ③ ④ ⑤

20

① ② ③ ④ ⑤

20

① ② ③ ④ ⑤

20

① ② ③ ④ ⑤

"When I think of the moments that have brought me the most pleasure, the most joy, they are almost always framed within the context of food and the table."

—STANLEY TUCCI

20 ⎤

① ② ③ ④ ⑤

20 ⎤

① ② ③ ④ ⑤

20 ⎤

① ② ③ ④ ⑤

20 ⎤

① ② ③ ④ ⑤

20 ⎤

① ② ③ ④ ⑤

"Food eaten at a table is better for you than food eaten hunched over a desk, standing at a counter, or driving in a car."

—PETER MAYLE

20

① ② ③ ④ ⑤

20

① ② ③ ④ ⑤

20

① ② ③ ④ ⑤

20

① ② ③ ④ ⑤

20

① ② ③ ④ ⑤

"We don't need to be professionals to cook well, any more than we need to be doctors to treat bruises and scrapes."

—TAMAR ADLER

20

① ② ③ ④ ⑤

20

① ② ③ ④ ⑤

20

① ② ③ ④ ⑤

20

① ② ③ ④ ⑤

20

① ② ③ ④ ⑤

"Only by growing some food for yourself can you become acquainted with the beautiful energy cycle that revolves from soil to seed to flower to fruit to food to offal to decay, and around again."

—WENDELL BERRY

20

① ② ③ ④ ⑤

20

① ② ③ ④ ⑤

20

① ② ③ ④ ⑤

20

① ② ③ ④ ⑤

20

① ② ③ ④ ⑤

MARCH
25

"Food is a big part of the home, and it brings people together—even if they don't want to be."

—NANCY MEYERS

20

① ② ③ ④ ⑤

20

① ② ③ ④ ⑤

20

① ② ③ ④ ⑤

20

① ② ③ ④ ⑤

20

① ② ③ ④ ⑤

"*I have come to realize that at some point in the day, I will order and consume a pizza so it might as well be in the morning.*"

—CHRISSY TEIGEN

20

①
②
③
④
⑤

20

①
②
③
④
⑤

20

①
②
③
④
⑤

20

①
②
③
④
⑤

20

①
②
③
④
⑤

"It doesn't matter if it's chicken and dumplings
or 'Oysters and Pearls' from The French Laundry.
If it's made with care, it is special."

—SEAN BROCK

20 _____

① ② ③ ④ ⑤

20 _____

① ② ③ ④ ⑤

20 _____

① ② ③ ④ ⑤

20 _____

① ② ③ ④ ⑤

20 _____

① ② ③ ④ ⑤

"When life gets more uncertain, more stressful than usual,
we look to foods that made us feel secure as children."

—MARIAN BURROS

20

①
②
③
④
⑤

20

①
②
③
④
⑤

20

①
②
③
④
⑤

20

①
②
③
④
⑤

20

①
②
③
④
⑤

MARCH

29

"Simple ingredients are often the most powerful."

—MICHEL BRAS

20 _____

①
②
③
④
⑤

20 _____

①
②
③
④
⑤

20 _____

①
②
③
④
⑤

20 _____

①
②
③
④
⑤

20 _____

①
②
③
④
⑤

"When people are eating the bread, breaking bread, there's a certain connective process between themselves and the product, as well as who's baking it."

—JONATHAN GOLDSMITH

MARCH
30

20 _____
_____ ①
_____ ②
_____ ③
_____ ④
_____ ⑤

20 _____
_____ ①
_____ ②
_____ ③
_____ ④
_____ ⑤

20 _____
_____ ①
_____ ②
_____ ③
_____ ④
_____ ⑤

20 _____
_____ ①
_____ ②
_____ ③
_____ ④
_____ ⑤

20 _____
_____ ①
_____ ②
_____ ③
_____ ④
_____ ⑤

"I believe with my whole heart in the act of cooking, in its smells, in its sounds, in its observable progress on the fire."

—MARCELLA HAZAN

20 _____

① _____
② _____
③ _____
④ _____
⑤ _____

20 _____

① _____
② _____
③ _____
④ _____
⑤ _____

20 _____

① _____
② _____
③ _____
④ _____
⑤ _____

20 _____

① _____
② _____
③ _____
④ _____
⑤ _____

20 _____

① _____
② _____
③ _____
④ _____
⑤ _____

"When I'm happy, I digest well."
—DEAN KOONTZ

20 _____
_____ ①
_____ ②
_____ ③
_____ ④
_____ ⑤

20 _____
_____ ①
_____ ②
_____ ③
_____ ④
_____ ⑤

20 _____
_____ ①
_____ ②
_____ ③
_____ ④
_____ ⑤

20 _____
_____ ①
_____ ②
_____ ③
_____ ④
_____ ⑤

20 _____
_____ ①
_____ ②
_____ ③
_____ ④
_____ ⑤

"My mother always told me, 'If you don't like the food you're served, just mess it up on the plate a bit.'"

—JOHN WATERS

20 ____

① ② ③ ④ ⑤

20 ____

① ② ③ ④ ⑤

20 ____

① ② ③ ④ ⑤

20 ____

① ② ③ ④ ⑤

20 ____

① ② ③ ④ ⑤

"The pleasures of dining well are not transitory, but abide forever."

—T.S. ELIOT

20

①
②
③
④
⑤

20

①
②
③
④
⑤

20

①
②
③
④
⑤

20

①
②
③
④
⑤

20

①
②
③
④
⑤

"Usually, when people are feeling stressed out they want a pill, but honey, give me a pot. For me, time in the kitchen is like time on the couch."

—PATTI LABELLE

20 _____ ① ② ③ ④ ⑤

20 _____ ① ② ③ ④ ⑤

20 _____ ① ② ③ ④ ⑤

20 _____ ① ② ③ ④ ⑤

20 _____ ① ② ③ ④ ⑤

"What is sauce for the goose may be sauce for the gander but is not necessarily sauce for the chicken, the duck, the turkey or the guinea hen."

—ALICE B. TOKLAS

20 ⌐

① ② ③ ④ ⑤

20 ⌐

① ② ③ ④ ⑤

20 ⌐

① ② ③ ④ ⑤

20 ⌐

① ② ③ ④ ⑤

20 ⌐

① ② ③ ④ ⑤

"It's not so easy to hate people with whom you're sharing good food."

—CARLA HALL

20 _____
① _____
② _____
_____
③ _____
④ _____
_____
⑤ _____

20 _____
① _____
② _____
_____
③ _____
④ _____
_____
⑤ _____

20 _____
① _____
② _____
_____
③ _____
④ _____
_____
⑤ _____

20 _____
① _____
② _____
_____
③ _____
④ _____
_____
⑤ _____

20 _____
① _____
② _____
_____
③ _____
④ _____
_____
⑤ _____

"Sadness and good food are incompatible."

—CHARLES SIMIC

20

①
②
③
④
⑤

20

①
②
③
④
⑤

20

①
②
③
④
⑤

20

①
②
③
④
⑤

20

①
②
③
④
⑤

APRIL

8

"One of the delights of life is eating with friends. Second to that is talking about eating. And, for an unsurpassed double whammy, there is talking about eating while you are eating with friends."
—LAURIE COLWIN

20

①
②
③
④
⑤

20

①
②
③
④
⑤

20

①
②
③
④
⑤

20

①
②
③
④
⑤

20

①
②
③
④
⑤

"When I am in trouble, eating is the only thing that consoles me. Indeed, when I am in really great trouble . . . I refuse everything except food and drink."

—OSCAR WILDE, *THE IMPORTANCE OF BEING EARNEST*

APRIL

9

20

① ② ③ ④ ⑤

20

① ② ③ ④ ⑤

20

① ② ③ ④ ⑤

20

① ② ③ ④ ⑤

20

① ② ③ ④ ⑤

APRIL

10

"Every time you try a new recipe it is like a new discovery, with all the adventure and excitement that goes along with that discovery."

—TAMMY WYNETTE

20 _____

① ___
② ___
③ ___
④ ___
⑤ ___

20 _____

① ___
② ___
③ ___
④ ___
⑤ ___

20 _____

① ___
② ___
③ ___
④ ___
⑤ ___

20 _____

① ___
② ___
③ ___
④ ___
⑤ ___

20 _____

① ___
② ___
③ ___
④ ___
⑤ ___

"There are only about five days a year that I don't have cheese, probably because I'm on an overnight plane going somewhere to eat cheese."

—LAURA WERLIN

20 ___

① ② ③ ④ ⑤

20 ___

① ② ③ ④ ⑤

20 ___

① ② ③ ④ ⑤

20 ___

① ② ③ ④ ⑤

20 ___

① ② ③ ④ ⑤

*"The most important things in life happen
over conversations while eating."*

—GEOFFREY ZAKARIAN

20 _____

① ② ③ ④ ⑤

20 _____

① ② ③ ④ ⑤

20 _____

① ② ③ ④ ⑤

20 _____

① ② ③ ④ ⑤

20 _____

① ② ③ ④ ⑤

"As we grow older we stop asking questions. And that's what science, and to a larger extent cooking should be about—challenging convention and asking questions."

—HESTON BLUMENTHAL

20 _____

_____
_____
_____
_____

① ② ③ ④ ⑤

20 _____

_____
_____
_____
_____

① ② ③ ④ ⑤

20 _____

_____
_____
_____
_____

① ② ③ ④ ⑤

20 _____

_____
_____
_____
_____

① ② ③ ④ ⑤

20 _____

_____
_____
_____
_____

① ② ③ ④ ⑤

APRIL

14

"I don't measure or fuss too much with details. How much of an ingredient? Enough for one good mess, a couple of handfuls or so. What size pan? Whatever I have handy."

—DORI SANDERS

20 _____

① ② ③ ④ ⑤

20 _____

① ② ③ ④ ⑤

20 _____

① ② ③ ④ ⑤

20 _____

① ② ③ ④ ⑤

20 _____

① ② ③ ④ ⑤

"Tourists, like armies, travel on their stomachs."

—VINCENT PRICE

20 _____

①
②
③
④
⑤

20 _____

①
②
③
④
⑤

20 _____

①
②
③
④
⑤

20 _____

①
②
③
④
⑤

20 _____

①
②
③
④
⑤

"I love hearing the expression 'Bon appétit!' But the two words I like even better: 'Let's cook!'"

—TED ALLEN

20 ___

① ___
② ___
③ ___
④ ___
⑤ ___

20 ___

① ___
② ___
③ ___
④ ___
⑤ ___

20 ___

① ___
② ___
③ ___
④ ___
⑤ ___

20 ___

① ___
② ___
③ ___
④ ___
⑤ ___

20 ___

① ___
② ___
③ ___
④ ___
⑤ ___

"The way you hold your knife and fork, ... and what you choose to put between them, determines so much about who you are, where you are from."

—GAIL SIMMONS

20

①
②
③
④
⑤

20

①
②
③
④
⑤

20

①
②
③
④
⑤

20

①
②
③
④
⑤

20

①
②
③
④
⑤

18

"Make food as nice for yourself as you would for guests."
—LAURA CALDER

20 _____

① ② ③ ④ ⑤

20 _____

① ② ③ ④ ⑤

20 _____

① ② ③ ④ ⑤

20 _____

① ② ③ ④ ⑤

20 _____

① ② ③ ④ ⑤

"With things like food, you approach life as it's actually lived, not in ideological or theoretical categories where everybody is distinct."

—FAREED ZAKARIA

20

① ② ③ ④ ⑤

20

① ② ③ ④ ⑤

20

① ② ③ ④ ⑤

20

① ② ③ ④ ⑤

20

① ② ③ ④ ⑤

"Are we making food fun enough for people? The food world has to let down its guard a little bit and stop being so . . . hoity-toity."

—ROY CHOI

20 _____

① ② ③ ④ ⑤

20 _____

① ② ③ ④ ⑤

20 _____

① ② ③ ④ ⑤

20 _____

① ② ③ ④ ⑤

20 _____

① ② ③ ④ ⑤

"When I don't have a bread going, I feel that something is missing. Could it be that I'm only completely happy now when a bread is happening somewhere?"

—ROSE LEVY BERANBAUM

20

① ② ③ ④ ⑤

20

① ② ③ ④ ⑤

20

① ② ③ ④ ⑤

20

① ② ③ ④ ⑤

20

① ② ③ ④ ⑤

"*I do not believe that what we eat can cure illness,
but I do believe that eating well and mindfully
can improve our sense of well-being.*"

—SEAMUS MULLEN

20

①
②
③
④
⑤

20

①
②
③
④
⑤

20

①
②
③
④
⑤

20

①
②
③
④
⑤

20

①
②
③
④
⑤

"Success in a kitchen is more like a marathon and less like a sprint."

—WYLIE DUFRESNE

20

① ② ③ ④ ⑤

20

① ② ③ ④ ⑤

20

① ② ③ ④ ⑤

20

① ② ③ ④ ⑤

20

① ② ③ ④ ⑤

APRIL

24

"The kitchen is the place where life, death, love, and hate all walk in and are rewarded or healed."

—PEARL BAILEY

20 ⎤

① ② ③ ④ ⑤

20 ⎤

① ② ③ ④ ⑤

20 ⎤

① ② ③ ④ ⑤

20 ⎤

① ② ③ ④ ⑤

20 ⎤

① ② ③ ④ ⑤

"Cooking is what makes us human."

—JONATHAN GOLD

APRIL

25

20 _____

① ②
③
④
⑤

20 _____

① ②
③
④
⑤

20 _____

① ②
③
④
⑤

20 _____

① ②
③
④
⑤

20 _____

① ②
③
④
⑤

"Good food should be joyful. There should be
laughter and chatter, not people sitting there like
they're in a funeral-parlor waiting room."

—JIM HARRISON

20 _____

①
②
③
④
⑤

20 _____

①
②
③
④
⑤

20 _____

①
②
③
④
⑤

20 _____

①
②
③
④
⑤

20 _____

①
②
③
④
⑤

"Giving someone a taste of something delicious at exactly the right moment is a fail-safe way to start a good relationship."
—KIM SEVERSON

APRIL
27

20 ___

① ___
② ___
③ ___
④ ___
⑤ ___

20 ___

① ___
② ___
③ ___
④ ___
⑤ ___

20 ___

① ___
② ___
③ ___
④ ___
⑤ ___

20 ___

① ___
② ___
③ ___
④ ___
⑤ ___

20 ___

① ___
② ___
③ ___
④ ___
⑤ ___

APRIL

28

"A food culture is not something that gets sold to people.
It arises out of a place, a soil, a climate, a history,
a temperament, a collective sense of belonging."

—BARBARA KINGSOLVER

20 ____

① ② ③ ④ ⑤

20 ____

① ② ③ ④ ⑤

20 ____

① ② ③ ④ ⑤

20 ____

① ② ③ ④ ⑤

20 ____

① ② ③ ④ ⑤

"At 6:30 we make it a point . . . no matter what the president is doing, we stop what we're doing, we sit down and and have a meal as a family."

—MICHELLE OBAMA

APRIL
29

20 _____

① ②
③
④
⑤

20 _____

① ②
③
④
⑤

20 _____

① ②
③
④
⑤

20 _____

① ②
③
④
⑤

20 _____

① ②
③
④
⑤

30

"When I cook things . . . I want to put it in the oven and . . .
take a bath. And I want to get out of the bathtub
25 minutes later, and I want it to be ready."

—DAVID SEDARIS

20 _____ ①
_____ ②
_____ ③
_____ ④
_____ ⑤

20 _____ ①
_____ ②
_____ ③
_____ ④
_____ ⑤

20 _____ ①
_____ ②
_____ ③
_____ ④
_____ ⑤

20 _____ ①
_____ ②
_____ ③
_____ ④
_____ ⑤

20 _____ ①
_____ ②
_____ ③
_____ ④
_____ ⑤

"Often I find that the least exciting way of cooking actually leads to the most wonderful place."

—APRIL BLOOMFIELD

20

① ② ③ ④ ⑤

20

① ② ③ ④ ⑤

20

① ② ③ ④ ⑤

20

① ② ③ ④ ⑤

20

① ② ③ ④ ⑤

"How do you make a soup without a can opener?
Well, that's a mystery of the trade to which very few
people know the answer. But it can be done."

—RAYMOND CHANDLER

20

① ② ③ ④ ⑤

20

① ② ③ ④ ⑤

20

① ② ③ ④ ⑤

20

① ② ③ ④ ⑤

20

① ② ③ ④ ⑤

"If what you eat is just mediocre, it will always leave you wanting."

—OPRAH WINFREY

20

① ② ③ ④ ⑤

20

① ② ③ ④ ⑤

20

① ② ③ ④ ⑤

20

① ② ③ ④ ⑤

20

① ② ③ ④ ⑤

MAY

4

"Viewing food as being about things other than bodily health—like pleasure, say, or socializing—makes people no less healthy; indeed, there's some reason to believe that it may make them more healthy."

—MICHAEL POLLAN

20

①
②
③
④
⑤

20

①
②
③
④
⑤

20

①
②
③
④
⑤

20

①
②
③
④
⑤

20

①
②
③
④
⑤

> "If you're out to learn something new, you will inevitably fail tremendously. Don't panic, stay cool. Then you eat it, move on, and next time you won't make the same mistake."
>
> —RENÉ REDZEPI

20

① ② ③ ④ ⑤

20

① ② ③ ④ ⑤

20

① ② ③ ④ ⑤

20

① ② ③ ④ ⑤

20

① ② ③ ④ ⑤

"Appreciate the whole process [of] cooking: chopping, smelling, tasting. It's like a moving meditation . . . once you really get into the groove, it calms you down."

—JOYCE GOLDSTEIN

20

① ② ③ ④ ⑤

20

① ② ③ ④ ⑤

20

① ② ③ ④ ⑤

20

① ② ③ ④ ⑤

20

① ② ③ ④ ⑤

"If there is a language that we all speak, it's food. And I think if it is possible for us to heal and not hate one another it will be through food."

—VIVIAN HOWARD

20

① ② ③ ④ ⑤

20

① ② ③ ④ ⑤

20

① ② ③ ④ ⑤

20

① ② ③ ④ ⑤

20

① ② ③ ④ ⑤

"Someone once asked what we talked about on long flights. 'Food!' we chorused. It's funny how much you look forward to the next meal when you're living out of a suitcase."

—HILLARY CLINTON

20 _____
① ② ③ ④ ⑤

20 _____
① ② ③ ④ ⑤

20 _____
① ② ③ ④ ⑤

20 _____
① ② ③ ④ ⑤

20 _____
① ② ③ ④ ⑤

"Eat a dinner, then eat a dinner after the dinner because it's usually not enough."

—ADAM DRIVER

20

①
②
③
④
⑤

20

①
②
③
④
⑤

20

①
②
③
④
⑤

20

①
②
③
④
⑤

20

①
②
③
④
⑤

10

"My role as a chef is respecting the produce. Why should I change and mask the original flavors of the produce that I'm utilizing?"

—JOËL ROBUCHON

20 _____

① ② ③ ④ ⑤

20 _____

① ② ③ ④ ⑤

20 _____

① ② ③ ④ ⑤

20 _____

① ② ③ ④ ⑤

20 _____

① ② ③ ④ ⑤

"It's not brain surgery what we do; it's cooking. I want to teach young people to just have a good time and not get caught up."

—DANIEL HUMM

20

① ② ③ ④ ⑤

20

① ② ③ ④ ⑤

20

① ② ③ ④ ⑤

20

① ② ③ ④ ⑤

20

① ② ③ ④ ⑤

*"Every now and then you encounter people who
say things like, 'I forgot to eat lunch today,' and
I always thought they were making it up."*

—EMMA STRAUB

20 ⬚

① ② ③ ④ ⑤

20 ⬚

① ② ③ ④ ⑤

20 ⬚

① ② ③ ④ ⑤

20 ⬚

① ② ③ ④ ⑤

20 ⬚

① ② ③ ④ ⑤

"My relationship with food is intimate. I don't eat and tell."
—CEELO GREEN

20

① ② ③ ④ ⑤

20

① ② ③ ④ ⑤

20

① ② ③ ④ ⑤

20

① ② ③ ④ ⑤

20

① ② ③ ④ ⑤

"You, the cook, must also be the artist, bringing understanding to mechanical formulas, transforming each into an uncomplicated statement that will surprise or soothe a gifted palate."

—RICHARD OLNEY

20 ____

① ② ③ ④ ⑤

20 ____

① ② ③ ④ ⑤

20 ____

① ② ③ ④ ⑤

20 ____

① ② ③ ④ ⑤

20 ____

① ② ③ ④ ⑤

"Food. I seldom think of anything else."
—TRUMAN CAPOTE

20

① ② ③ ④ ⑤

20

① ② ③ ④ ⑤

20

① ② ③ ④ ⑤

20

① ② ③ ④ ⑤

20

① ② ③ ④ ⑤

"Cooking was a way of questioning and asking myself why things were the way they were."

—FERRAN ADRIÀ

20 _____

① ② ③ ④ ⑤

20 _____

① ② ③ ④ ⑤

20 _____

① ② ③ ④ ⑤

20 _____

① ② ③ ④ ⑤

20 _____

① ② ③ ④ ⑤

"'Going out' means going out to dinner. It's about the conversation: someone recognizing your intellect, the charm of flirting, and really speaking to somebody."

—KERI RUSSELL

20

①
②
③
④
⑤

20

①
②
③
④
⑤

20

①
②
③
④
⑤

20

①
②
③
④
⑤

20

①
②
③
④
⑤

MAY

18

"It's not that people shouldn't be serious about pizza, but it's no more important than other things in life like being kind to people and trying to be a good person."

—CHRIS BIANCO

20

① ② ③ ④ ⑤

20

① ② ③ ④ ⑤

20

① ② ③ ④ ⑤

20

① ② ③ ④ ⑤

20

① ② ③ ④ ⑤

"The best sauce in the world is hunger."

—MIGUEL DE CERVANTES, *DON QUIXOTE*

20 ⌐

①
②
③
④
⑤

20 ⌐

①
②
③
④
⑤

20 ⌐

①
②
③
④
⑤

20 ⌐

①
②
③
④
⑤

20 ⌐

①
②
③
④
⑤

"It's a cliché, but cliches are often true: the best dishes are the simplest."

—HANYA YANAGIHARA

20

① ② ③ ④ ⑤

20

① ② ③ ④ ⑤

20

① ② ③ ④ ⑤

20

① ② ③ ④ ⑤

20

① ② ③ ④ ⑤

"I cannot eat and think about restriction. When I eat, I eat. I do not understand the idea of guilty pleasure. It's all about pleasure."

—ERIC RIPERT

MAY
21

---

20 |

① ② ③ ④ ⑤

---

20 |

① ② ③ ④ ⑤

---

20 |

① ② ③ ④ ⑤

---

20 |

① ② ③ ④ ⑤

---

20 |

① ② ③ ④ ⑤

*"Surely there is no more exquisite jointure
in the anatomy of life than that at which
poetry dovetails with the inevitable meal."*

—MARY BARNARD, "REMARKS ON POETRY AND THE PHYSICAL WORLD"

20 ⎤

① ② ③ ④ ⑤

20 ⎤

① ② ③ ④ ⑤

20 ⎤

① ② ③ ④ ⑤

20 ⎤

① ② ③ ④ ⑤

20 ⎤

① ② ③ ④ ⑤

"If it's not literally a perfect custard, but you have maintained a great feeling for it, then you have created a recipe perfectly because there was that passion behind what you did."

—THOMAS KELLER

MAY

23

20 ⌐
_____
_____
_____
_____
_____

①
②
③
④
⑤

20 ⌐
_____
_____
_____
_____
_____

①
②
③
④
⑤

20 ⌐
_____
_____
_____
_____
_____

①
②
③
④
⑤

20 ⌐
_____
_____
_____
_____
_____

①
②
③
④
⑤

20 ⌐
_____
_____
_____
_____
_____

①
②
③
④
⑤

24

"I often find myself thinking about what I will eat at my next meal while I'm in the middle of eating a meal."

—JIM GAFFIGAN

20 _____

① ② ③ ④ ⑤

20 _____

① ② ③ ④ ⑤

20 _____

① ② ③ ④ ⑤

20 _____

① ② ③ ④ ⑤

20 _____

① ② ③ ④ ⑤

"Get out of your comfort zone. If you're going to make the same thing over and over again, you really need to buy some new condiments."

—MELISSA CLARK

20

① ② ③ ④ ⑤

20

① ② ③ ④ ⑤

20

① ② ③ ④ ⑤

20

① ② ③ ④ ⑤

20

① ② ③ ④ ⑤

*"There's still food, but I don't want to eat it.
I've become everything I ever hated!"*

—HOMER SIMPSON, *THE SIMPSONS*

20 _____ ①
_____ ②
_____ ③
_____ ④
_____ ⑤

20 _____ ①
_____ ②
_____ ③
_____ ④
_____ ⑤

20 _____ ①
_____ ②
_____ ③
_____ ④
_____ ⑤

20 _____ ①
_____ ②
_____ ③
_____ ④
_____ ⑤

20 _____ ①
_____ ②
_____ ③
_____ ④
_____ ⑤

"I think it's important in our [food] industry to be curious. To go to places where you don't usually go. To see places that you don't usually see. Not to stay in your comfort zone."

—DOMINIQUE ANSEL

MAY

27

20 _____

① _____
② _____
③ _____
④ _____
⑤ _____

20 _____

① _____
② _____
③ _____
④ _____
⑤ _____

20 _____

① _____
② _____
③ _____
④ _____
⑤ _____

20 _____

① _____
② _____
③ _____
④ _____
⑤ _____

20 _____

① _____
② _____
③ _____
④ _____
⑤ _____

"*I was so worried I baked a whole cake.
And then I ate a whole cake.*"

—LINCOLN RICE, *BROAD CITY*

20 _____

① ②③④⑤

20 _____

① ②③④⑤

20 _____

① ②③④⑤

20 _____

① ②③④⑤

20 _____

① ②③④⑤

"Good cooking is the result of a balance struck between frugality and liberality."

—PATIENCE GRAY

20 ⌐

① ② ③ ④ ⑤

20 ⌐

① ② ③ ④ ⑤

20 ⌐

① ② ③ ④ ⑤

20 ⌐

① ② ③ ④ ⑤

20 ⌐

① ② ③ ④ ⑤

MAY

30

"Cooking is a love affair. It's all about falling in love with your ingredients."

—ALAIN DUCASSE

20 ____

① ____
② ____
③ ____
④ ____
⑤ ____

20 ____

① ____
② ____
③ ____
④ ____
⑤ ____

20 ____

① ____
② ____
③ ____
④ ____
⑤ ____

20 ____

① ____
② ____
③ ____
④ ____
⑤ ____

20 ____

① ____
② ____
③ ____
④ ____
⑤ ____

"In a bad marriage you have different quarrels every day and in a good marriage you have the same quarrels every day and it's usually about food."

—ADAM GOPNIK

20

① ② ③ ④ ⑤

20

① ② ③ ④ ⑤

20

① ② ③ ④ ⑤

20

① ② ③ ④ ⑤

20

① ② ③ ④ ⑤

*"We want everything we make to taste
of what we used to make it."*

—ELISABETH PRUEITT

20

① ② ③ ④ ⑤

20

① ② ③ ④ ⑤

20

① ② ③ ④ ⑤

20

① ② ③ ④ ⑤

20

① ② ③ ④ ⑤

"*I love cheese plates. Though I actually hate cheese plates. Because I can't say no to them.*"

—SETH MEYERS

20

① ② ③ ④ ⑤

20

① ② ③ ④ ⑤

20

① ② ③ ④ ⑤

20

① ② ③ ④ ⑤

20

① ② ③ ④ ⑤

3

"As for butter versus margarine, I trust cows more than chemists."
—JOAN GUSSOW

20 _____

① _____
② _____
③ _____
④ _____
⑤ _____

20 _____

① _____
② _____
③ _____
④ _____
⑤ _____

20 _____

① _____
② _____
③ _____
④ _____
⑤ _____

20 _____

① _____
② _____
③ _____
④ _____
⑤ _____

20 _____

① _____
② _____
③ _____
④ _____
⑤ _____

"I always serve myself first. I convince myself that it makes my guests feel comfortable."

—JONATHAN ADLER

20

① ② ③ ④ ⑤

20

① ② ③ ④ ⑤

20

① ② ③ ④ ⑤

20

① ② ③ ④ ⑤

20

① ② ③ ④ ⑤

"There's real magic in a box of instant Jell-O, one that can't be matched with egg yolks and butter, and you've got to respect your roots more than your training to admit it."

—STELLA PARKS

20 |

① ② ③ ④ ⑤

20 |

① ② ③ ④ ⑤

20 |

① ② ③ ④ ⑤

20 |

① ② ③ ④ ⑤

20 |

① ② ③ ④ ⑤

"Give me Books, fruit, French wine and fine weather and a little music out of doors, played by somebody I do not know."

—JOHN KEATS

20 ____

① ____
② ____
③ ____
④ ____
⑤ ____

20 ____

① ____
② ____
③ ____
④ ____
⑤ ____

20 ____

① ____
② ____
③ ____
④ ____
⑤ ____

20 ____

① ____
② ____
③ ____
④ ____
⑤ ____

20 ____

① ____
② ____
③ ____
④ ____
⑤ ____

"*Laugh they did, and eat, and drink, often and heartily, being fond of simple jests at all times, and of six meals a day (when they could get them).*"

—J.R.R. TOLKIEN, *THE FELLOWSHIP OF THE RING*

20

① ② ③ ④ ⑤

20

① ② ③ ④ ⑤

20

① ② ③ ④ ⑤

20

① ② ③ ④ ⑤

20

① ② ③ ④ ⑤

"I'm attracted to pie. It doesn't mean I feel the need to date pie."
—LORELAI GILMORE, *GILMORE GIRLS*

20

① ② ③ ④ ⑤

20

① ② ③ ④ ⑤

20

① ② ③ ④ ⑤

20

① ② ③ ④ ⑤

20

① ② ③ ④ ⑤

JUNE

"Creating begins in the marketplace. What I see starts me thinking about flavors and textures, combinations and balance."

—TOM COLICCHIO

20

① ② ③ ④ ⑤

20

① ② ③ ④ ⑤

20

① ② ③ ④ ⑤

20

① ② ③ ④ ⑤

20

① ② ③ ④ ⑤

"If you can understand a culture, then you understand the food.
If you can understand the food, you understand the people."

—EMERIL LAGASSE

20

① ② ③ ④ ⑤

20

① ② ③ ④ ⑤

20

① ② ③ ④ ⑤

20

① ② ③ ④ ⑤

20

① ② ③ ④ ⑤

JUNE

11

"They're not Picasso, after all—this is supper. So I don't want to hear about a chef's intentions. Call me when it's good."

—MIMI SHERATON

20

① ② ③ ④ ⑤

20

① ② ③ ④ ⑤

20

① ② ③ ④ ⑤

20

① ② ③ ④ ⑤

20

① ② ③ ④ ⑤

> "A French writer once said 'a recipe has a hidden side, like the moon.' In every recipe there's a little something that makes it special, and, hopefully, better."
>
> —PAULA WOLFERT

JUNE

12

20

① ② ③ ④ ⑤

20

① ② ③ ④ ⑤

20

① ② ③ ④ ⑤

20

① ② ③ ④ ⑤

20

① ② ③ ④ ⑤

"God made food, the devil the cooks."
—JAMES JOYCE, *ULYSSES*

20 ⌐

① ② ③ ④ ⑤

20 ⌐

① ② ③ ④ ⑤

20 ⌐

① ② ③ ④ ⑤

20 ⌐

① ② ③ ④ ⑤

20 ⌐

① ② ③ ④ ⑤

"I think of equipment as kind of an impediment to touching and tasting and being engaged with our food in a meaningful and inspired way."

—ALICE WATERS

20 ____

①
②
③
④
⑤

20 ____

①
②
③
④
⑤

20 ____

①
②
③
④
⑤

20 ____

①
②
③
④
⑤

20 ____

①
②
③
④
⑤

15

"Technique, no matter how humble the dish, is important."
—CHARLES PHAN

20 ⎞
_____ ①
_____ ②
_____ ③
_____ ④
_____ ⑤

20 ⎞
_____ ①
_____ ②
_____ ③
_____ ④
_____ ⑤

20 ⎞
_____ ①
_____ ②
_____ ③
_____ ④
_____ ⑤

20 ⎞
_____ ①
_____ ②
_____ ③
_____ ④
_____ ⑤

20 ⎞
_____ ①
_____ ②
_____ ③
_____ ④
_____ ⑤

> *"All you needed to know about any human society was what they ate. If you knew what they ate you could deduce everything else—culture, philosophy, morals, politics, everything."*
>
> —REX STOUT, *THE FINAL DEDUCTION*

JUNE

16

20 ⌐

_____
①
②
③
④
⑤

20 ⌐

_____
①
②
③
④
⑤

20 ⌐

_____
①
②
③
④
⑤

20 ⌐

_____
①
②
③
④
⑤

20 ⌐

_____
①
②
③
④
⑤

17

"I saw that a man could devote his life to baking bread, and that it was a good life, a worthy profession and one to be revered."

—SEBASTIEN ROUXEL

20 ⬚
1
2
3
4
5

20 ⬚
1
2
3
4
5

20 ⬚
1
2
3
4
5

20 ⬚
1
2
3
4
5

20 ⬚
1
2
3
4
5

"An almost messianic fervor is characteristic of many great cooks, no matter what their nationality."

—ANNE WILLAN

JUNE

18

20

① ② ③ ④ ⑤

20

① ② ③ ④ ⑤

20

① ② ③ ④ ⑤

20

① ② ③ ④ ⑤

20

① ② ③ ④ ⑤

19

"If you are what you eat, then I only want to eat the good stuff."
—REMY, *RATATOUILLE*

20 ____

① ____
② ____
③ ____
④ ____
⑤ ____

20 ____

① ____
② ____
③ ____
④ ____
⑤ ____

20 ____

① ____
② ____
③ ____
④ ____
⑤ ____

20 ____

① ____
② ____
③ ____
④ ____
⑤ ____

20 ____

① ____
② ____
③ ____
④ ____
⑤ ____

"I ate another apple pie and ice cream; that's practically all I ate all the way across the country. I knew it was nutritious and it was delicious, of course."

—JACK KEROUAC, *ON THE ROAD*

20 ⌐

① ② ③ ④ ⑤

20 ⌐

① ② ③ ④ ⑤

20 ⌐

① ② ③ ④ ⑤

20 ⌐

① ② ③ ④ ⑤

20 ⌐

① ② ③ ④ ⑤

"There's something beautiful about taking an ugly vegetable, cooking it simply, and turning it into an insanely tasty dish."

—ALEX GUARNASCHELLI

20 _____

① _____
② _____
③ _____
④ _____
⑤ _____

20 _____

① _____
② _____
③ _____
④ _____
⑤ _____

20 _____

① _____
② _____
③ _____
④ _____
⑤ _____

20 _____

① _____
② _____
③ _____
④ _____
⑤ _____

20 _____

① _____
② _____
③ _____
④ _____
⑤ _____

"The best thing you can have in a kitchen is confidence. I really think that's what separates good cooks from the mediocre ones."

—GORDON RAMSAY

20

① ② ③ ④ ⑤

20

① ② ③ ④ ⑤

20

① ② ③ ④ ⑤

20

① ② ③ ④ ⑤

20

① ② ③ ④ ⑤

"When you've cooked that steak a thousand times, it will tell you what you need to know. You have to listen to it."

—RICK BAYLESS

20

① ② ③ ④ ⑤

20

① ② ③ ④ ⑤

20

① ② ③ ④ ⑤

20

① ② ③ ④ ⑤

20

① ② ③ ④ ⑤

"Good food has the power to make the moment."

—AYESHA CURRY

20 ⌐

① ② ③ ④ ⑤

20 ⌐

① ② ③ ④ ⑤

20 ⌐

① ② ③ ④ ⑤

20 ⌐

① ② ③ ④ ⑤

20 ⌐

① ② ③ ④ ⑤

JUNE
25

"I believe it's a cook's moral obligation to add more butter given the chance."

—MICHAEL RUHLMAN

20 _____
- ① _____
- ② _____
- ③ _____
- ④ _____
- ⑤ _____

20 _____
- ① _____
- ② _____
- ③ _____
- ④ _____
- ⑤ _____

20 _____
- ① _____
- ② _____
- ③ _____
- ④ _____
- ⑤ _____

20 _____
- ① _____
- ② _____
- ③ _____
- ④ _____
- ⑤ _____

20 _____
- ① _____
- ② _____
- ③ _____
- ④ _____
- ⑤ _____

"*Long after I've forgotten the names of monuments, train stations, or boulevards of a city I've traveled to, the flavors would stay with me.*"

—HEIDI SWANSON

20

① ② ③ ④ ⑤

20

① ② ③ ④ ⑤

20

① ② ③ ④ ⑤

20

① ② ③ ④ ⑤

20

① ② ③ ④ ⑤

JUNE

27

"Music wishes it was food. Music cries itself to sleep over not having been born a ripe fig or a shank of lamb."
—STEVE ALBINI

20

①
②
③
④
⑤

20

①
②
③
④
⑤

20

①
②
③
④
⑤

20

①
②
③
④
⑤

20

①
②
③
④
⑤

"It's about making something out of nothing: manipulating fruit or vegetables to turn them into something else is extremely gratifying."

—BROOKS HEADLEY

20 _____

① _____
② _____
③ _____
④ _____
⑤ _____

20 _____

① _____
② _____
③ _____
④ _____
⑤ _____

20 _____

① _____
② _____
③ _____
④ _____
⑤ _____

20 _____

① _____
② _____
③ _____
④ _____
⑤ _____

20 _____

① _____
② _____
③ _____
④ _____
⑤ _____

29

"A really delicious sugary treat is my version of pure joy."
—SAMANTHA BEE

20 _____

① ② ③ ④ ⑤

20 _____

① ② ③ ④ ⑤

20 _____

① ② ③ ④ ⑤

20 _____

① ② ③ ④ ⑤

20 _____

① ② ③ ④ ⑤

*"Very well, I will marry you if you promise
not to make me eat eggplant."*

—GABRIEL GARCÍA-MÁRQUEZ, *LOVE IN THE TIME OF CHOLERA*

20 ___

① ___
② ___
③ ___
④ ___
⑤ ___

20 ___

① ___
② ___
③ ___
④ ___
⑤ ___

20 ___

① ___
② ___
③ ___
④ ___
⑤ ___

20 ___

① ___
② ___
③ ___
④ ___
⑤ ___

20 ___

① ___
② ___
③ ___
④ ___
⑤ ___

JULY

1

"Every culinary choice that we make defines who we are—not just to ourselves, but also to theirs."

—SYBIL KAPOOR

20 _____
_____
_____
_____
_____
① ② ③ ④ ⑤

20 _____
_____
_____
_____
_____
① ② ③ ④ ⑤

20 _____
_____
_____
_____
_____
① ② ③ ④ ⑤

20 _____
_____
_____
_____
_____
① ② ③ ④ ⑤

20 _____
_____
_____
_____
_____
① ② ③ ④ ⑤

"Eating is essential to life, and it is a pleasure that we can share with friends. . . . It should be a happy experience, not a torturous trial."

—JENNIFER MCLAGAN

20

① ② ③ ④ ⑤

20

① ② ③ ④ ⑤

20

① ② ③ ④ ⑤

20

① ② ③ ④ ⑤

20

① ② ③ ④ ⑤

"The most underused tool in the kitchen is the brain. . . . We don't think about recipes as much as we perform them."

—ALTON BROWN

20 _____
_____ ①
_____ ②
_____ ③
_____ ④
_____ ⑤

20 _____
_____ ①
_____ ②
_____ ③
_____ ④
_____ ⑤

20 _____
_____ ①
_____ ②
_____ ③
_____ ④
_____ ⑤

20 _____
_____ ①
_____ ②
_____ ③
_____ ④
_____ ⑤

20 _____
_____ ①
_____ ②
_____ ③
_____ ④
_____ ⑤

"I think cooking is the way to everyone's heart. There is an emotionality about cooking, an intimacy, a breaking of barriers and ice."

—ROCCO DISPIRITO

JULY

4

20 _____

① ___
② ___
③ ___
④ ___
⑤ ___

20 _____

① ___
② ___
③ ___
④ ___
⑤ ___

20 _____

① ___
② ___
③ ___
④ ___
⑤ ___

20 _____

① ___
② ___
③ ___
④ ___
⑤ ___

20 _____

① ___
② ___
③ ___
④ ___
⑤ ___

5

"I could never get enough attention, enough love, or enough peanut butter."

—GAEL GREENE

20 _____

① ② ③ ④ ⑤

20 _____

① ② ③ ④ ⑤

20 _____

① ② ③ ④ ⑤

20 _____

① ② ③ ④ ⑤

20 _____

① ② ③ ④ ⑤

"Cuisine is a medium for the expression of history."
—OLIVIER ROELLINGER

20

① ② ③ ④ ⑤

20

① ② ③ ④ ⑤

20

① ② ③ ④ ⑤

20

① ② ③ ④ ⑤

20

① ② ③ ④ ⑤

"The transformation of humble ingredients into delightful desserts inspires people to exclaim with joy following a single bite."

—JOANNE CHANG

20

① ② ③ ④ ⑤

20

① ② ③ ④ ⑤

20

① ② ③ ④ ⑤

20

① ② ③ ④ ⑤

20

① ② ③ ④ ⑤

"A pianist told me that she perfected recipes the way she perfected pieces of music, repeating them over and over until she got it right."

—PATRICIA WELLS

8

20

① ② ③ ④ ⑤

20

① ② ③ ④ ⑤

20

① ② ③ ④ ⑤

20

① ② ③ ④ ⑤

20

① ② ③ ④ ⑤

"He who distinguishes the true savor of his food can never be a glutton."

—HENRY DAVID THOREAU

20

① ② ③ ④ ⑤

20

① ② ③ ④ ⑤

20

① ② ③ ④ ⑤

20

① ② ③ ④ ⑤

20

① ② ③ ④ ⑤

"You're only as good as your last dish."
—WES AVILA

20 _____

①
②
③
④
⑤

20 _____

①
②
③
④
⑤

20 _____

①
②
③
④
⑤

20 _____

①
②
③
④
⑤

20 _____

①
②
③
④
⑤

"The most amazing dining experiences are less about the restaurants and more about who you're with, the time of your life, the arc of your memories."

—TRACI DES JARDINS

20 _____
① _____
② _____
③ _____
④ _____
⑤ _____

20 _____
① _____
② _____
③ _____
④ _____
⑤ _____

20 _____
① _____
② _____
③ _____
④ _____
⑤ _____

20 _____
① _____
② _____
③ _____
④ _____
⑤ _____

20 _____
① _____
② _____
③ _____
④ _____
⑤ _____

"Baked a lemon meringue pie, cooled lemon custard & crust on cold bathroom windowsill, stirring in black night & stars. . . . Shaping a meal, people, I grew back to joy."

—SYLVIA PLATH

JULY

12

20

①
②
③
④
⑤

20

①
②
③
④
⑤

20

①
②
③
④
⑤

20

①
②
③
④
⑤

20

①
②
③
④
⑤

13

"Think of cooking as an outlet for your ideas, a release for the artist in you."

—WOLFGANG PUCK

20

① ② ③ ④ ⑤

20

① ② ③ ④ ⑤

20

① ② ③ ④ ⑤

20

① ② ③ ④ ⑤

20

① ② ③ ④ ⑤

> "Taste . . . is always a compound emotion, made up of
> what we read, what we want, and what we taste."
>
> —ADAM GOPNIK

20

① ② ③ ④ ⑤

20

① ② ③ ④ ⑤

20

① ② ③ ④ ⑤

20

① ② ③ ④ ⑤

20

① ② ③ ④ ⑤

"For me, the most vivid meals have been the ones I've always fallen into or that have included a surprise twist to the story."

—PETER HOFFMAN

20 _____ ① ② ③ ④ ⑤

20 _____ ① ② ③ ④ ⑤

20 _____ ① ② ③ ④ ⑤

20 _____ ① ② ③ ④ ⑤

20 _____ ① ② ③ ④ ⑤

"I used to say that I was a foodie, but then my wife pointed out, after she went to culinary school, that I'm just someone who likes to eat a lot."

—TY BURRELL

20

①
②
③
④
⑤

20

①
②
③
④
⑤

20

①
②
③
④
⑤

20

①
②
③
④
⑤

20

①
②
③
④
⑤

"In cooking there are crucial moments that you need to understand and realize. You don't just leave it there and go do something else."

—LIDIA BASTIANICH

20

① ② ③ ④ ⑤

20

① ② ③ ④ ⑤

20

① ② ③ ④ ⑤

20

① ② ③ ④ ⑤

20

① ② ③ ④ ⑤

"We may live without friends; we may live without books; but civilized man cannot live without cooks."

—OWEN MEREDITH

JULY

18

20

①
②
③
④
⑤

20

①
②
③
④
⑤

20

①
②
③
④
⑤

20

①
②
③
④
⑤

20

①
②
③
④
⑤

19

"Food is the first thing. Morals follow on."
—BERTOLT BRECHT, *THE THREEPENNY OPERA*

20

① ② ③ ④ ⑤

20

① ② ③ ④ ⑤

20

① ② ③ ④ ⑤

20

① ② ③ ④ ⑤

20

① ② ③ ④ ⑤

"If you like good food, why not honor yourself enough to make a pleasing meal and relish every mouthful?"

—JUDITH JONES

20 _____

① ② ③ ④ ⑤

20 _____

① ② ③ ④ ⑤

20 _____

① ② ③ ④ ⑤

20 _____

① ② ③ ④ ⑤

20 _____

① ② ③ ④ ⑤

"A knife is not like a car that breaks down. If it does not perform, you have not kept it sharp. Remember, it is never the knife's fault."

—DANIEL BOULUD

20

① ② ③ ④ ⑤

20

① ② ③ ④ ⑤

20

① ② ③ ④ ⑤

20

① ② ③ ④ ⑤

20

① ② ③ ④ ⑤

"We exchanged recipes as we would precious gifts."
—CLAUDIA RODEN

20

①
②
③
④
⑤

20

①
②
③
④
⑤

20

①
②
③
④
⑤

20

①
②
③
④
⑤

20

①
②
③
④
⑤

JULY

23

"Any cuisine that is not evolving is dying."
—RICK BAYLESS

20 _____ ①
_____ ②
_____ ③
_____ ④
_____ ⑤

20 _____ ①
_____ ②
_____ ③
_____ ④
_____ ⑤

20 _____ ①
_____ ②
_____ ③
_____ ④
_____ ⑤

20 _____ ①
_____ ②
_____ ③
_____ ④
_____ ⑤

20 _____ ①
_____ ②
_____ ③
_____ ④
_____ ⑤

"Good food is what I live on, not fine language."
—MOLIÈRE, *LEARNED LADIES*

20 ____

①
②
③
④
⑤

20 ____

①
②
③
④
⑤

20 ____

①
②
③
④
⑤

20 ____

①
②
③
④
⑤

20 ____

①
②
③
④
⑤

JULY

25

"Making a cake . . . knowing all those smiles that await you, has a kind of hidden social agenda—it's cheaper than therapy and much more pleasurable."

—DELIA SMITH

20 _____

①
②
③
④
⑤

20 _____

①
②
③
④
⑤

20 _____

①
②
③
④
⑤

20 _____

①
②
③
④
⑤

20 _____

①
②
③
④
⑤

"I like to think that I eat like man and cry like a little baby."

—TIMOTHY OLYPHANT

20 _____

① ② ③ ④ ⑤

20 _____

① ② ③ ④ ⑤

20 _____

① ② ③ ④ ⑤

20 _____

① ② ③ ④ ⑤

20 _____

① ② ③ ④ ⑤

27

"It's not about learning a recipe—it's about learning how to taste."

—JEREMY FOX

20 _____

① ② ③ ④ ⑤

20 _____

① ② ③ ④ ⑤

20 _____

① ② ③ ④ ⑤

20 _____

① ② ③ ④ ⑤

20 _____

① ② ③ ④ ⑤

"The smell of food cooking, your mother's or father's voice, the clang of the utensils, and the taste of the food: These memories will stay with you for the rest of your life."

—JACQUES PÉPIN

20 _____

① _____
② _____
③ _____
④ _____
⑤ _____

20 _____

① _____
② _____
③ _____
④ _____
⑤ _____

20 _____

① _____
② _____
③ _____
④ _____
⑤ _____

20 _____

① _____
② _____
③ _____
④ _____
⑤ _____

20 _____

① _____
② _____
③ _____
④ _____
⑤ _____

29

"Good food, properly cooked, gives us good blood, sound bones, healthy brains, strong nerves, and firm flesh, to say nothing of good tempers and kind hearts."

—JULIET CORSON

20

① ② ③ ④ ⑤

20

① ② ③ ④ ⑤

20

① ② ③ ④ ⑤

20

① ② ③ ④ ⑤

20

① ② ③ ④ ⑤

"My mom used to say that a gift should be something a person doesn't need, and although she meant clothes and jewelry, I think she could have been talking about baking."

—DORIE GREENSPAN

20

①
②
③
④
⑤

20

①
②
③
④
⑤

20

①
②
③
④
⑤

20

①
②
③
④
⑤

20

①
②
③
④
⑤

"Just give me all the bacon and eggs you have."

—RON SWANSON, *PARKS AND RECREATION*

20 _____

① ② ③ ④ ⑤

20 _____

① ② ③ ④ ⑤

20 _____

① ② ③ ④ ⑤

20 _____

① ② ③ ④ ⑤

20 _____

① ② ③ ④ ⑤

"No matter how difficult family relations might be, if someone cooks a meal with real care and love it makes everyone feel good."

—JOSCELINE DIMBLEBY

20

①
②
③
④
⑤

20

①
②
③
④
⑤

20

①
②
③
④
⑤

20

①
②
③
④
⑤

20

①
②
③
④
⑤

"More pasta and less panache."

—MARIO PUZO

20

① ② ③ ④ ⑤

20

① ② ③ ④ ⑤

20

① ② ③ ④ ⑤

20

① ② ③ ④ ⑤

20

① ② ③ ④ ⑤

"In the world of food, new and cool is often rated but actually, predictable food done well is amazing."

—JAMIE OLIVER

AUGUST

3

20 _____

① _____
② _____
③ _____
④ _____
⑤ _____

20 _____

① _____
② _____
③ _____
④ _____
⑤ _____

20 _____

① _____
② _____
③ _____
④ _____
⑤ _____

20 _____

① _____
② _____
③ _____
④ _____
⑤ _____

20 _____

① _____
② _____
③ _____
④ _____
⑤ _____

"Anybody with a terminally jangled lifestyle needs at least one psychic anchor every twenty-four hours, and mine is breakfast."
—HUNTER S. THOMPSON

20

①
②
③
④
⑤

20

①
②
③
④
⑤

20

①
②
③
④
⑤

20

①
②
③
④
⑤

20

①
②
③
④
⑤

"It's so much more than just cooking: it's about learning while you cook, and pushing the boundaries of what you know so that you can grow and move forward."

—JOSÉ ANDRÉS

20

① ② ③ ④ ⑤

20

① ② ③ ④ ⑤

20

① ② ③ ④ ⑤

20

① ② ③ ④ ⑤

20

① ② ③ ④ ⑤

"Excess in too little has ever proved in me more dangerous than the excess in too much; the last may cause indigestion, but the first causes death."

—GIACOMO CASANOVA

20 _____ ① ② ③ ④ ⑤

20 _____ ① ② ③ ④ ⑤

20 _____ ① ② ③ ④ ⑤

20 _____ ① ② ③ ④ ⑤

20 _____ ① ② ③ ④ ⑤

*"Flavor is the stimulation: it's your emotional,
historical, intellectual charge to something."*

—MICHAEL CHIARELLO

AUGUST

7

20

① ② ③ ④ ⑤

20

① ② ③ ④ ⑤

20

① ② ③ ④ ⑤

20

① ② ③ ④ ⑤

20

① ② ③ ④ ⑤

8

"Cooking is one of the most beautiful gifts you can give to someone. It embodies love, patience, and balance."

—BRIAN GROSZ

20

① ② ③ ④ ⑤

20

① ② ③ ④ ⑤

20

① ② ③ ④ ⑤

20

① ② ③ ④ ⑤

20

① ② ③ ④ ⑤

"To me, at that moment, food was more than food: it was words, and it was the memory of music, and it was the memory of old television shows."

—QUESTLOVE

AUGUST

9

20

①
②
③
④
⑤

20

①
②
③
④
⑤

20

①
②
③
④
⑤

20

①
②
③
④
⑤

20

①
②
③
④
⑤

"Ice cream encourages you to be in the moment. It's melting and changing each second—you have to pay attention to it, or it disappears."

—JENI BRITTON BAUER

20 _____
① _____
② _____
③ _____
④ _____
⑤ _____

20 _____
① _____
② _____
③ _____
④ _____
⑤ _____

20 _____
① _____
② _____
③ _____
④ _____
⑤ _____

20 _____
① _____
② _____
③ _____
④ _____
⑤ _____

20 _____
① _____
② _____
③ _____
④ _____
⑤ _____

"I always think of a custodian. Or a fisherman or a rancher or a farmer. Whatever they produce or collect or gather, I don't wanna screw it up too much."

—JONATHAN WAXMAN

AUGUST
11

20

① ② ③ ④ ⑤

20

① ② ③ ④ ⑤

20

① ② ③ ④ ⑤

20

① ② ③ ④ ⑤

20

① ② ③ ④ ⑤

"*Kissing don't last: cookery do!*"
—GEORGE MEREDITH, *THE ORDEAL OF RICHARD FEVEREL*

20

① ② ③ ④ ⑤

20

① ② ③ ④ ⑤

20

① ② ③ ④ ⑤

20

① ② ③ ④ ⑤

20

① ② ③ ④ ⑤

"90 percent of women spend 61 minutes a day doubting food, doubting their choices, wondering what I'm going to eat next. Who has time for that? That equates to 15 days out of a year. I don't have time to do that!"
—TARAJI P. HENSON

20

① \
② \
③ \
④ \
⑤

20

① \
② \
③ \
④ \
⑤

20

① \
② \
③ \
④ \
⑤

20

① \
② \
③ \
④ \
⑤

20

① \
② \
③ \
④ \
⑤

"One can say everything best over a meal."
—GEORGE ELIOT, *ADAM BEDE*

20

① ② ③ ④ ⑤

20

① ② ③ ④ ⑤

20

① ② ③ ④ ⑤

20

① ② ③ ④ ⑤

20

① ② ③ ④ ⑤

"My life-defining relationship, after all, wasn't with a parent,
a sibling, a teacher, a mate. It was with my stomach."

—FRANK BRUNI

20

① ② ③ ④ ⑤

20

① ② ③ ④ ⑤

20

① ② ③ ④ ⑤

20

① ② ③ ④ ⑤

20

① ② ③ ④ ⑤

"I cannot look at a fruit bowl without thinking of the universe. Minus the bananas, there aren't many banana-shaped things in the universe."

—NEIL DEGRASSE TYSON

20

①
②
③
④
⑤

20

①
②
③
④
⑤

20

①
②
③
④
⑤

20

①
②
③
④
⑤

20

①
②
③
④
⑤

"To feed without a friend is the life of a lion and a wolf."
—EPICURUS

AUGUST
17

20

① ② ③ ④ ⑤

20

① ② ③ ④ ⑤

20

① ② ③ ④ ⑤

20

① ② ③ ④ ⑤

20

① ② ③ ④ ⑤

18

"The most important ingredient . . . for a chef is culture."
—MASSIMO BOTTURA

20 _____

① ____
② ____
③ ____
④ ____
⑤ ____

20 _____

① ____
② ____
③ ____
④ ____
⑤ ____

20 _____

① ____
② ____
③ ____
④ ____
⑤ ____

20 _____

① ____
② ____
③ ____
④ ____
⑤ ____

20 _____

① ____
② ____
③ ____
④ ____
⑤ ____

"Life within doors has few pleasanter prospects than a neatly-arranged and well-provisioned breakfast-table."

—NATHANIEL HAWTHORNE, *THE HOUSE OF THE SEVEN GABLES*

AUGUST

19

20

① ② ③ ④ ⑤

20

① ② ③ ④ ⑤

20

① ② ③ ④ ⑤

20

① ② ③ ④ ⑤

20

① ② ③ ④ ⑤

"Food doesn't really talk back to you, you know? It's offering you love, which is great. It's like a dog in that way."

—JAMI ATTENBERG

20 _____

① _____
② _____
③ _____
④ _____
⑤ _____

20 _____

① _____
② _____
③ _____
④ _____
⑤ _____

20 _____

① _____
② _____
③ _____
④ _____
⑤ _____

20 _____

① _____
② _____
③ _____
④ _____
⑤ _____

20 _____

① _____
② _____
③ _____
④ _____
⑤ _____

"The only reason I work out is to live longer so I can eat more cheese and drink more wine."

—RICKY GERVAIS

AUGUST
21

20

① ② ③ ④ ⑤

20

① ② ③ ④ ⑤

20

① ② ③ ④ ⑤

20

① ② ③ ④ ⑤

20

① ② ③ ④ ⑤

"I think what helps us to achieve [communion] is the dishes that we grew up with, the dishes that are familiar, the dishes that have always meant solidarity and family."

—JUNOT DÍAZ

20

① ② ③ ④ ⑤

20

① ② ③ ④ ⑤

20

① ② ③ ④ ⑤

20

① ② ③ ④ ⑤

20

① ② ③ ④ ⑤

"There are only two activities that every people group
on earth wants to do in a group.... We want to
laugh together, and we want to eat together."

—ALTON BROWN

20

① ② ③ ④ ⑤

20

① ② ③ ④ ⑤

20

① ② ③ ④ ⑤

20

① ② ③ ④ ⑤

20

① ② ③ ④ ⑤

"Those who do not enjoy eating seldom have much capacity for enjoyment or usefulness of any sort."
—CHARLES W. ELIOT

20 _____
_____ ①
_____ ②
_____ ③
_____ ④
_____ ⑤

20 _____
_____ ①
_____ ②
_____ ③
_____ ④
_____ ⑤

20 _____
_____ ①
_____ ②
_____ ③
_____ ④
_____ ⑤

20 _____
_____ ①
_____ ②
_____ ③
_____ ④
_____ ⑤

20 _____
_____ ①
_____ ②
_____ ③
_____ ④
_____ ⑤

"Food should be about love—not about competition."

—SÉBASTIEN BRAS

20

① ② ③ ④ ⑤

20

① ② ③ ④ ⑤

20

① ② ③ ④ ⑤

20

① ② ③ ④ ⑤

20

① ② ③ ④ ⑤

"Food is the core of society—when people want to communicate something positive they will communicate it through food."

—DOMINIQUE CRENN

20 _____
① ___
② ___
③ ___
④ ___
⑤ ___

20 _____
① ___
② ___
③ ___
④ ___
⑤ ___

20 _____
① ___
② ___
③ ___
④ ___
⑤ ___

20 _____
① ___
② ___
③ ___
④ ___
⑤ ___

20 _____
① ___
② ___
③ ___
④ ___
⑤ ___

"There is an opportunity to learn something new every day, taste something new every day, read something new every day."

—MICHAEL LAISKONIS

20

① ② ③ ④ ⑤

20

① ② ③ ④ ⑤

20

① ② ③ ④ ⑤

20

① ② ③ ④ ⑤

20

① ② ③ ④ ⑤

"Homer never wrote on an empty stomach."

—FRANÇOIS RABELAIS

20 _____

①
②
③
④
⑤

20 _____

①
②
③
④
⑤

20 _____

①
②
③
④
⑤

20 _____

①
②
③
④
⑤

20 _____

①
②
③
④
⑤

"Whenever I stop at a restaurant while traveling, I go and look at the chef. If he's a thin fellow, I don't eat there."

—FERNAND POINT

20

① ② ③ ④ ⑤

20

① ② ③ ④ ⑤

20

① ② ③ ④ ⑤

20

① ② ③ ④ ⑤

20

① ② ③ ④ ⑤

"*I never feel guilty for eating or drinking something I like!*"
—AMANDA HESSER

20 _____

①
②
③
④
⑤

20 _____

①
②
③
④
⑤

20 _____

①
②
③
④
⑤

20 _____

①
②
③
④
⑤

20 _____

①
②
③
④
⑤

"At the end of the day, cooking is much more than techniques: it's an art de vivre."

—ALAIN DUCASSE

20 _____

① _____
② _____
③ _____
④ _____
⑤ _____

20 _____

① _____
② _____
③ _____
④ _____
⑤ _____

20 _____

① _____
② _____
③ _____
④ _____
⑤ _____

20 _____

① _____
② _____
③ _____
④ _____
⑤ _____

20 _____

① _____
② _____
③ _____
④ _____
⑤ _____

"I never like to eat anything that's looking at me."
—JOHNNY CARSON

20 _____ ①
_____ ②
_____ ③
_____ ④
_____ ⑤

20 _____ ①
_____ ②
_____ ③
_____ ④
_____ ⑤

20 _____ ①
_____ ②
_____ ③
_____ ④
_____ ⑤

20 _____ ①
_____ ②
_____ ③
_____ ④
_____ ⑤

20 _____ ①
_____ ②
_____ ③
_____ ④
_____ ⑤

"Food is not destined to be good or destined to be bad—it is what you do to it or what you do not do to it that affects the results."

—JUDY RODGERS

SEPTEMBER

2

20

① ② ③ ④ ⑤

20

① ② ③ ④ ⑤

20

① ② ③ ④ ⑤

20

① ② ③ ④ ⑤

20

① ② ③ ④ ⑤

"Our diet, like that of the birds, must answer to the season."
—HENRY DAVID THOREAU

20

① ② ③ ④ ⑤

20

① ② ③ ④ ⑤

20

① ② ③ ④ ⑤

20

① ② ③ ④ ⑤

20

① ② ③ ④ ⑤

"I'll have what she's having."

—WOMAN AT KATZ'S DELI, *WHEN HARRY MET SALLY*

20

①
②
③
④
⑤

20

①
②
③
④
⑤

20

①
②
③
④
⑤

20

①
②
③
④
⑤

20

①
②
③
④
⑤

"*Its filling sequestered beneath a canopy of top crust, hidden from the eye (if not the nose) a pie (not unlike the body) offers itself for reverie on the enigma of inside and out.*"

—JUDITH MOORE

20 ___

① ② ③ ④ ⑤

20 ___

① ② ③ ④ ⑤

20 ___

① ② ③ ④ ⑤

20 ___

① ② ③ ④ ⑤

20 ___

① ② ③ ④ ⑤

"Just do one dish over and over until you get it right—that will help you build confidence."

—ALICE WATERS

20

① ② ③ ④ ⑤

20

① ② ③ ④ ⑤

20

① ② ③ ④ ⑤

20

① ② ③ ④ ⑤

20

① ② ③ ④ ⑤

"Serious cooking is an essentially optimistic act.
It reaches into the future, vanishes into memory,
and creates the desire for another meal."

—ELIZABETH EHRLICH

20

① ② ③ ④ ⑤

20

① ② ③ ④ ⑤

20

① ② ③ ④ ⑤

20

① ② ③ ④ ⑤

20

① ② ③ ④ ⑤

"We do not eat for the good of living, but because the meat is savory and the appetite is keen."

—RALPH WALDO EMERSON

SEPTEMBER
8

20 _____
_____
_____
_____
_____
① ② ③ ④ ⑤

20 _____
_____
_____
_____
_____
① ② ③ ④ ⑤

20 _____
_____
_____
_____
_____
① ② ③ ④ ⑤

20 _____
_____
_____
_____
_____
① ② ③ ④ ⑤

20 _____
_____
_____
_____
_____
① ② ③ ④ ⑤

"If the chef is an artist, he doesn't succeed. Why? Because he is inspired today but not tomorrow."

—ANDRÉ SOLTNER

20

① ② ③ ④ ⑤

20

① ② ③ ④ ⑤

20

① ② ③ ④ ⑤

20

① ② ③ ④ ⑤

20

① ② ③ ④ ⑤

"The stories were often in some way about food, and the food always turned out to be about something much larger: grace, difference, faith, love."

—DIANA ABU-JABER

20

① ② ③ ④ ⑤

20

① ② ③ ④ ⑤

20

① ② ③ ④ ⑤

20

① ② ③ ④ ⑤

20

① ② ③ ④ ⑤

"Cooking is like love. It should be entered into with abandon or not at all."

—HARRIET VAN HORNE

20

① ② ③ ④ ⑤

20

① ② ③ ④ ⑤

20

① ② ③ ④ ⑤

20

① ② ③ ④ ⑤

20

① ② ③ ④ ⑤

"When you eat something that's really good you say, 'I can die, now.'"

—ENRIQUE OLVERA

SEPTEMBER
12

20

①
②
③
④
⑤

20

①
②
③
④
⑤

20

①
②
③
④
⑤

20

①
②
③
④
⑤

20

①
②
③
④
⑤

"My mother made food to mirror our mood,
food for the weary and melancholy."

—JHUMPA LAHIRI

20

① ② ③ ④ ⑤

20

① ② ③ ④ ⑤

20

① ② ③ ④ ⑤

20

① ② ③ ④ ⑤

20

① ② ③ ④ ⑤

*"Interesting is not enough. Food must
be pleasurable and delicious."*

—PAUL LIEBRANDT

20 _____

① ② ③ ④ ⑤

20 _____

① ② ③ ④ ⑤

20 _____

① ② ③ ④ ⑤

20 _____

① ② ③ ④ ⑤

20 _____

① ② ③ ④ ⑤

"Part of the secret of success in life is to eat what you like and let the food fight it out inside."

—MARK TWAIN

20

① ② ③ ④ ⑤

20

① ② ③ ④ ⑤

20

① ② ③ ④ ⑤

20

① ② ③ ④ ⑤

20

① ② ③ ④ ⑤

"No one who has never eaten a food to excess has ever really experienced it, or fully exposed himself to it."

—WALTER BENJAMIN

20

①
②
③
④
⑤

20

①
②
③
④
⑤

20

①
②
③
④
⑤

20

①
②
③
④
⑤

20

①
②
③
④
⑤

"Men have always believed that there was something mysterious and difficult about making a pie. Here is a great secret. There is nothing to it."

—ERNEST HEMINGWAY

20 _____

① ②
③ ④
⑤

20 _____

① ②
③ ④
⑤

20 _____

① ②
③ ④
⑤

20 _____

① ②
③ ④
⑤

20 _____

① ②
③ ④
⑤

"For with their understated display of wealth, [onions] bring you to one of the oldest and most secret things of the world: the sight of what no one but you has ever seen."

—ROBERT FARRAR CAPON

20

① ② ③ ④ ⑤

20

① ② ③ ④ ⑤

20

① ② ③ ④ ⑤

20

① ② ③ ④ ⑤

20

① ② ③ ④ ⑤

"Bread is the only food I know that satisfies completely, all by itself. It comforts the body, charms the senses, gratifies the soul, and excites the mind. A little butter also helps."

—JEFFREY STEINGARTEN

20

① ② ③ ④ ⑤

20

① ② ③ ④ ⑤

20

① ② ③ ④ ⑤

20

① ② ③ ④ ⑤

20

① ② ③ ④ ⑤

"*I always think the worst thing you can do to cooking is give a disclaimer. . . . There's nothing to apologize for.*"

—JULIA TURSHEN

20 _____

① ② ③ ④ ⑤

20 _____

① ② ③ ④ ⑤

20 _____

① ② ③ ④ ⑤

20 _____

① ② ③ ④ ⑤

20 _____

① ② ③ ④ ⑤

SEPTEMBER
21

"If language didn't arise at mealtimes, it certainly evolved and became more fluent there."

—DIANE ACKERMAN

20 _____

① ② ③ ④ ⑤

20 _____

① ② ③ ④ ⑤

20 _____

① ② ③ ④ ⑤

20 _____

① ② ③ ④ ⑤

20 _____

① ② ③ ④ ⑤

"Any meal shared around a table—the life lived inside each course—is only as good as the intimacies among people there."

—MICHAEL PATERNITI

20

① ② ③ ④ ⑤

20

① ② ③ ④ ⑤

20

① ② ③ ④ ⑤

20

① ② ③ ④ ⑤

20

① ② ③ ④ ⑤

23

"I find cooking to be a meditative experience. And it's one
of the ways I nourish myself and show myself love."

—TRACEE ELLIS ROSS

20 _____

① ② ③ ④ ⑤

20 _____

① ② ③ ④ ⑤

20 _____

① ② ③ ④ ⑤

20 _____

① ② ③ ④ ⑤

20 _____

① ② ③ ④ ⑤

"*Food is never just something to eat.*"

—MARGARET VISSER

20

①
②
③
④
⑤

20

①
②
③
④
⑤

20

①
②
③
④
⑤

20

①
②
③
④
⑤

20

①
②
③
④
⑤

SEPTEMBER
25

"Culture begins when the raw gets cooked."
—FELIPE FERNÁNDEZ-ARMESTO

20

① ② ③ ④ ⑤

20

① ② ③ ④ ⑤

20

① ② ③ ④ ⑤

20

① ② ③ ④ ⑤

20

① ② ③ ④ ⑤

*"There are certain things that just make
you happy. Food makes me happy."*
—PATTI SMITH

20

① ② ③ ④ ⑤

20

① ② ③ ④ ⑤

20

① ② ③ ④ ⑤

20

① ② ③ ④ ⑤

20

① ② ③ ④ ⑤

"A recipe is just a story that ends with a good meal."
—PAT CONROY

20

① ② ③ ④ ⑤

20

① ② ③ ④ ⑤

20

① ② ③ ④ ⑤

20

① ② ③ ④ ⑤

20

① ② ③ ④ ⑤

"I cannot believe that the world would not be a better world
if we reflected on it after a really advantageous dinner."
—WALLACE STEVENS

SEPTEMBER

28

20

①
②
③
④
⑤

20

①
②
③
④
⑤

20

①
②
③
④
⑤

20

①
②
③
④
⑤

20

①
②
③
④
⑤

"It is only in company that eating is done justice; food must be divided and distributed if it is to be well received."

—WALTER BENJAMIN

20 ⌐

① ② ③ ④ ⑤

20 ⌐

① ② ③ ④ ⑤

20 ⌐

① ② ③ ④ ⑤

20 ⌐

① ② ③ ④ ⑤

20 ⌐

① ② ③ ④ ⑤

"A man seldom thinks with more earnestness of any thing than he does of his dinner."

—SAMUEL JOHNSON

20

①
②
③
④
⑤

20

①
②
③
④
⑤

20

①
②
③
④
⑤

20

①
②
③
④
⑤

20

①
②
③
④
⑤

"Every meal should be a small celebration."

—FANNIE FARMER

20 _____

① ② ③ ④ ⑤

20 _____

① ② ③ ④ ⑤

20 _____

① ② ③ ④ ⑤

20 _____

① ② ③ ④ ⑤

20 _____

① ② ③ ④ ⑤

*"Who knows if a well-prepared soup was not responsible
for the pneumatic pump or a poor one for a war?"*

—GEORG CHRISTOPH LICHTENBERG

OCTOBER

2

20 ⎤
① ② ③ ④ ⑤

20 ⎤
① ② ③ ④ ⑤

20 ⎤
① ② ③ ④ ⑤

20 ⎤
① ② ③ ④ ⑤

20 ⎤
① ② ③ ④ ⑤

"Good food is always a trouble and its preparation
should be regarded as a labour of love."

—ELIZABETH DAVID

20

① ② ③ ④ ⑤

20

① ② ③ ④ ⑤

20

① ② ③ ④ ⑤

20

① ② ③ ④ ⑤

20

① ② ③ ④ ⑤

"Everyone has a story and a recipe. We cherish them because they are our reinventions. Our recipes convey who we were, are, and want to be."

—EDWARD LEE

OCTOBER

4

20 ____

① ② ③ ④ ⑤

20 ____

① ② ③ ④ ⑤

20 ____

① ② ③ ④ ⑤

20 ____

① ② ③ ④ ⑤

20 ____

① ② ③ ④ ⑤

"The guest will judge better of a feast than the cook."

—ARISTOTLE

20 ⎤
①
②
③
④
⑤

20 ⎤
①
②
③
④
⑤

20 ⎤
①
②
③
④
⑤

20 ⎤
①
②
③
④
⑤

20 ⎤
①
②
③
④
⑤

"All of humankind has one thing in common: the sandwich. I believe that all anyone really wants in this life is to sit in peace and eat a sandwich."

—LIZ LEMON, *30 ROCK*

OCTOBER

6

20 ⎹

① ② ③ ④ ⑤

20 ⎹

① ② ③ ④ ⑤

20 ⎹

① ② ③ ④ ⑤

20 ⎹

① ② ③ ④ ⑤

20 ⎹

① ② ③ ④ ⑤

"Taste is a soothsayer, a truth teller."

—DAN BARBER

20

① ② ③ ④ ⑤

20

① ② ③ ④ ⑤

20

① ② ③ ④ ⑤

20

① ② ③ ④ ⑤

20

① ② ③ ④ ⑤

"That man is no friend who does not give of his own nourishment to his friend, the companion at his side."

—RIGVEDA

OCTOBER

8

20 |

①
②
③
④
⑤

20 |

①
②
③
④
⑤

20 |

①
②
③
④
⑤

20 |

①
②
③
④
⑤

20 |

①
②
③
④
⑤

*"Hunger makes you restless. You dream about food—
not just any food, but perfect food, the best food,
magical meals, famous and awe-inspiring."*

—DOROTHY ALLISON, *BASTARD OUT OF CAROLINA*

20

① ② ③ ④ ⑤

20

① ② ③ ④ ⑤

20

① ② ③ ④ ⑤

20

① ② ③ ④ ⑤

20

① ② ③ ④ ⑤

"There is a history of food, but it's also the
most ephemeral of the performing arts."

—NATHAN MYHRVOLD

20

① ② ③ ④ ⑤

20

① ② ③ ④ ⑤

20

① ② ③ ④ ⑤

20

① ② ③ ④ ⑤

20

① ② ③ ④ ⑤

"Without the assistance of both [eating and drinking], the most sparkling wit would be as heavy as a bad soufflé, and the brightest talent as dull as my looking-glass on a foggy day."

—ALEXIS SOYER

20

① ② ③ ④ ⑤

20

① ② ③ ④ ⑤

20

① ② ③ ④ ⑤

20

① ② ③ ④ ⑤

20

① ② ③ ④ ⑤

"Unquiet meals make ill digestions."

—WILLIAM SHAKESPEARE, *A COMEDY OF ERRORS*

20

① ② ③ ④ ⑤

20

① ② ③ ④ ⑤

20

① ② ③ ④ ⑤

20

① ② ③ ④ ⑤

20

① ② ③ ④ ⑤

"The kitchen spoke to me of my childhood, family, and whole life."

—SOPHIA LOREN

20 _____

① ② ③ ④ ⑤

20 _____

① ② ③ ④ ⑤

20 _____

① ② ③ ④ ⑤

20 _____

① ② ③ ④ ⑤

20 _____

① ② ③ ④ ⑤

"It is just as absurd to exact excellent cooking from a chef whom one provides with defective or scanty goods, as to hope to obtain wine from a bottled decoction of logwood."

—AUGUSTE ESCOFFIER

20 _____
_____ ①
_____ ②
_____ ③
_____ ④
_____ ⑤

20 _____
_____ ①
_____ ②
_____ ③
_____ ④
_____ ⑤

20 _____
_____ ①
_____ ②
_____ ③
_____ ④
_____ ⑤

20 _____
_____ ①
_____ ②
_____ ③
_____ ④
_____ ⑤

20 _____
_____ ①
_____ ②
_____ ③
_____ ④
_____ ⑤

"Of soup and love, the first is the best."

—THOMAS FULLER

20

① ② ③ ④ ⑤

20

① ② ③ ④ ⑤

20

① ② ③ ④ ⑤

20

① ② ③ ④ ⑤

20

① ② ③ ④ ⑤

"One of the very nicest things about life is the way we must regularly stop whatever it is we are doing and devote our attention to eating."

—LUCIANO PAVAROTTI

20

① ② ③ ④ ⑤

20

① ② ③ ④ ⑤

20

① ② ③ ④ ⑤

20

① ② ③ ④ ⑤

20

① ② ③ ④ ⑤

"When I cook, I always imagine I'm in front of a stretch of blank canvas. The dishes I paint, so to speak, must be a vibrant and energetic balance of color and flavor."

—NOBUYUKI MATSUHISA

20 ⎤

    ① ② ③ ④ ⑤

20 ⎤

    ① ② ③ ④ ⑤

20 ⎤

    ① ② ③ ④ ⑤

20 ⎤

    ① ② ③ ④ ⑤

20 ⎤

    ① ② ③ ④ ⑤

*"The spirituality of man is most apparent
when he is eating a hearty dinner."*

—W. SOMERSET MAUGHAM

20 ⌐

①
②
③
④
⑤

20 ⌐

①
②
③
④
⑤

20 ⌐

①
②
③
④
⑤

20 ⌐

①
②
③
④
⑤

20 ⌐

①
②
③
④
⑤

"There's a point where people get into the zone and something clicks for them, where they fall in love with cooking."
—MOLLIE KATZEN

20

① ② ③ ④ ⑤

20

① ② ③ ④ ⑤

20

① ② ③ ④ ⑤

20

① ② ③ ④ ⑤

20

① ② ③ ④ ⑤

"A cuisine is not shaped so much by its consumers as they, again in the most literal sense, are shaped by it."

—WAVERLEY ROOT

20

①
②
③
④
⑤

20

①
②
③
④
⑤

20

①
②
③
④
⑤

20

①
②
③
④
⑤

20

①
②
③
④
⑤

"All cooking is cooking for comfort."

—RUTH REICHL

20 _____
_____ ①
_____ ②
_____ ③
_____ ④
_____ ⑤

20 _____
_____ ①
_____ ②
_____ ③
_____ ④
_____ ⑤

20 _____
_____ ①
_____ ②
_____ ③
_____ ④
_____ ⑤

20 _____
_____ ①
_____ ②
_____ ③
_____ ④
_____ ⑤

20 _____
_____ ①
_____ ②
_____ ③
_____ ④
_____ ⑤

> "I count my cooking by the looks of satisfaction on the faces of the people who have eaten my food. I don't want them to be impressed; I want them to be pleased."
>
> —ANDRÉ SOLTNER

20 _____
_____
_____
_____
_____

① ② ③ ④ ⑤

20 _____
_____
_____
_____
_____

① ② ③ ④ ⑤

20 _____
_____
_____
_____
_____

① ② ③ ④ ⑤

20 _____
_____
_____
_____
_____

① ② ③ ④ ⑤

20 _____
_____
_____
_____
_____

① ② ③ ④ ⑤

"You can eat anything at any time. Who made the rule that you have to have eggs in the morning, and steak at night?"

—MAYA ANGELOU

20 ____

①
②
③
④
⑤

20 ____

①
②
③
④
⑤

20 ____

①
②
③
④
⑤

20 ____

①
②
③
④
⑤

20 ____

①
②
③
④
⑤

"What's better than comfort food with someone that you love?"

—JACQUES TORRES

20 _____

① _____
② _____
③ _____
④ _____
⑤ _____

20 _____

① _____
② _____
③ _____
④ _____
⑤ _____

20 _____

① _____
② _____
③ _____
④ _____
⑤ _____

20 _____

① _____
② _____
③ _____
④ _____
⑤ _____

20 _____

① _____
② _____
③ _____
④ _____
⑤ _____

"It is impossible not to love someone who makes toast for you."

—NIGEL SLATER

20

① ② ③ ④ ⑤

20

① ② ③ ④ ⑤

20

① ② ③ ④ ⑤

20

① ② ③ ④ ⑤

20

① ② ③ ④ ⑤

"A well-rounded life begins with a well-balanced meal."

—DAPHNE OZ

20

① ② ③ ④ ⑤

20

① ② ③ ④ ⑤

20

① ② ③ ④ ⑤

20

① ② ③ ④ ⑤

20

① ② ③ ④ ⑤

"I like putting new tastes in my mouth. I like the adventure. Soon we'll all be dead; that's my mantra. . . . Soon I won't be able to taste something new. So I don't like to waste meals."

—DAVID SIMON

20

① ② ③ ④ ⑤

20

① ② ③ ④ ⑤

20

① ② ③ ④ ⑤

20

① ② ③ ④ ⑤

20

① ② ③ ④ ⑤

"My approach to cooking has always been 'Why not?'"
—JOE CARROLL

20

① ② ③ ④ ⑤

20

① ② ③ ④ ⑤

20

① ② ③ ④ ⑤

20

① ② ③ ④ ⑤

20

① ② ③ ④ ⑤

*"A good piece of chicken can make anybody
believe in the existence of God."*

—SHERMAN ALEXIE, *THE ABSOLUTELY TRUE DIARY OF A PART-TIME INDIAN*

20

①
②
③
④
⑤

20

①
②
③
④
⑤

20

①
②
③
④
⑤

20

①
②
③
④
⑤

20

①
②
③
④
⑤

*"Good cooking, in the final analysis, depends on
two things: common sense and good taste."*

—SIMON HOPKINSON

20 ⌐

① ② ③ ④ ⑤

20 ⌐

① ② ③ ④ ⑤

20 ⌐

① ② ③ ④ ⑤

20 ⌐

① ② ③ ④ ⑤

20 ⌐

① ② ③ ④ ⑤

"I see food as ingredients and something to satisfy. It looks as good as it is."

—FERGUS HENDERSON

20 _____
① ② ③ ④ ⑤

20 _____
① ② ③ ④ ⑤

20 _____
① ② ③ ④ ⑤

20 _____
① ② ③ ④ ⑤

20 _____
① ② ③ ④ ⑤

"My favorite dessert is whatever is chocolate and is near."

—MAIDA HEATTER

20 _____

① _____
② _____
③ _____
④ _____
⑤ _____

20 _____

① _____
② _____
③ _____
④ _____
⑤ _____

20 _____

① _____
② _____
③ _____
④ _____
⑤ _____

20 _____

① _____
② _____
③ _____
④ _____
⑤ _____

20 _____

① _____
② _____
③ _____
④ _____
⑤ _____

"Sometimes it is the only worthwhile product you can salvage from a day: what you make to eat."

—JOHN IRVING, *THE WORLD ACCORDING TO GARP*

20

① ② ③ ④ ⑤

20

① ② ③ ④ ⑤

20

① ② ③ ④ ⑤

20

① ② ③ ④ ⑤

20

① ② ③ ④ ⑤

*"As long as food comes from nature herself,
I don't see why you shouldn't eat it."*

—MICHEL GUÉRARD

NOVEMBER

3

20

①
②
③
④
⑤

20

①
②
③
④
⑤

20

①
②
③
④
⑤

20

①
②
③
④
⑤

20

①
②
③
④
⑤

"The people that view food solely as nourishment are behind the times. Food can be expressive and therefore food can be art."

—GRANT ACHATZ

20

① ② ③ ④ ⑤

20

① ② ③ ④ ⑤

20

① ② ③ ④ ⑤

20

① ② ③ ④ ⑤

20

① ② ③ ④ ⑤

"I don't like to eat alone. I have to associate the idea of someone with the things that please me."

—GUSTAVE FLAUBERT

20 ____

① ____
② ____
③ ____
④ ____
⑤ ____

20 ____

① ____
② ____
③ ____
④ ____
⑤ ____

20 ____

① ____
② ____
③ ____
④ ____
⑤ ____

20 ____

① ____
② ____
③ ____
④ ____
⑤ ____

20 ____

① ____
② ____
③ ____
④ ____
⑤ ____

*"Eggs are not just the symbol of life, they are
the most magical of all ingredients."*

—RAYMOND BLANC

20 _____

① _____
② _____
③ _____
④ _____
⑤ _____

20 _____

① _____
② _____
③ _____
④ _____
⑤ _____

20 _____

① _____
② _____
③ _____
④ _____
⑤ _____

20 _____

① _____
② _____
③ _____
④ _____
⑤ _____

20 _____

① _____
② _____
③ _____
④ _____
⑤ _____

"I really think that the only reason to have food and wine is to have better conversation—with your wife, your lover, your peers, your children, whoever is sitting with you."

—FRANCIS MALLMAN

NOVEMBER

7

20

① ② ③ ④ ⑤

20

① ② ③ ④ ⑤

20

① ② ③ ④ ⑤

20

① ② ③ ④ ⑤

20

① ② ③ ④ ⑤

"*Almost every person has something secret he likes to eat.*"
—M.F.K. FISHER

20

① ② ③ ④ ⑤

20

① ② ③ ④ ⑤

20

① ② ③ ④ ⑤

20

① ② ③ ④ ⑤

20

① ② ③ ④ ⑤

*"In my family you never greeted someone with 'how are you?';
it was always 'chr le ma?' which means 'have you eaten?'"*

—MING TSAI

20 ___

① ___
② ___
③ ___
④ ___
⑤ ___

20 ___

① ___
② ___
③ ___
④ ___
⑤ ___

20 ___

① ___
② ___
③ ___
④ ___
⑤ ___

20 ___

① ___
② ___
③ ___
④ ___
⑤ ___

20 ___

① ___
② ___
③ ___
④ ___
⑤ ___

NOVEMBER

10

"Breakfast is a peaceful moment for me, so I never have the radio on, no music, no noise around. The only noise that is permitted is people's voices."

—CHRISTIAN LOUBOUTIN

20 _____

① _____
② _____
③ _____
④ _____
⑤ _____

20 _____

① _____
② _____
③ _____
④ _____
⑤ _____

20 _____

① _____
② _____
③ _____
④ _____
⑤ _____

20 _____

① _____
② _____
③ _____
④ _____
⑤ _____

20 _____

① _____
② _____
③ _____
④ _____
⑤ _____

"Romanticism could not quench my need for food. Even Baudelaire had to eat."

—PATTI SMITH

NOVEMBER

11

20 _____

① _____
② _____
③ _____
④ _____
⑤ _____

20 _____

① _____
② _____
③ _____
④ _____
⑤ _____

20 _____

① _____
② _____
③ _____
④ _____
⑤ _____

20 _____

① _____
② _____
③ _____
④ _____
⑤ _____

20 _____

① _____
② _____
③ _____
④ _____
⑤ _____

"I went looking for food not simply to satisfy my palate, but to experience enlightenment, or a flash of recollection, or to understand a tradition and make it known to others."

—UMBERTO ECO

20

① ② ③ ④ ⑤

20

① ② ③ ④ ⑤

20

① ② ③ ④ ⑤

20

① ② ③ ④ ⑤

20

① ② ③ ④ ⑤

"Every meal is a chance to entertain, an idea that often gets lost in the planning, preparation, execution, and excitement."

—MAGNUS NILSSON

20

① ② ③ ④ ⑤

20

① ② ③ ④ ⑤

20

① ② ③ ④ ⑤

20

① ② ③ ④ ⑤

20

① ② ③ ④ ⑤

"Clean plates don't lie."

—DAN BARBER

20

① ② ③ ④ ⑤

20

① ② ③ ④ ⑤

20

① ② ③ ④ ⑤

20

① ② ③ ④ ⑤

20

① ② ③ ④ ⑤

"It's only after a bit of breakfast that I'm able to regard the world with that sunny cheeriness which makes a fellow a universal favourite."

—P.G. WODEHOUSE, "JEEVES AND THE UNBIDDEN GUEST"

NOVEMBER

15

20 ___

① ___
② ___
③ ___
④ ___
⑤ ___

20 ___

① ___
② ___
③ ___
④ ___
⑤ ___

20 ___

① ___
② ___
③ ___
④ ___
⑤ ___

20 ___

① ___
② ___
③ ___
④ ___
⑤ ___

20 ___

① ___
② ___
③ ___
④ ___
⑤ ___

"When you acknowledge, as you must, that there is no such
thing as perfect food, only the idea of it, then the real purpose of
striving toward perfection becomes clear: to make people happy."

—THOMAS KELLER

20 ⌐

① ② ③ ④ ⑤

20 ⌐

① ② ③ ④ ⑤

20 ⌐

① ② ③ ④ ⑤

20 ⌐

① ② ③ ④ ⑤

20 ⌐

① ② ③ ④ ⑤

"Most of all there were books and food, food and books, both excellent things."

—GERTRUDE STEIN

20 ⌐

①
②
③
④
⑤

20 ⌐

①
②
③
④
⑤

20 ⌐

①
②
③
④
⑤

20 ⌐

①
②
③
④
⑤

20 ⌐

①
②
③
④
⑤

NOVEMBER
18

*"The one thing that makes a soufflé fall is
letting it know you are afraid of it."*

—JAMES BEARD

20 _____
①
②
③
④
⑤

20 _____
①
②
③
④
⑤

20 _____
①
②
③
④
⑤

20 _____
①
②
③
④
⑤

20 _____
①
②
③
④
⑤

"Often, whenever I come up against anything painful or difficult, my mind escapes to food."

—KATE CHRISTENSEN

NOVEMBER
19

20

① ② ③ ④ ⑤

20

① ② ③ ④ ⑤

20

① ② ③ ④ ⑤

20

① ② ③ ④ ⑤

20

① ② ③ ④ ⑤

"What my aunt Alia took pleasure in: cooking. What she had, during the lonely madness of the years, raised to the level of an art-form: the impregnation of food with emotions."

—SALMAN RUSHDIE, *MIDNIGHT'S CHILDREN*

20

① ② ③ ④ ⑤

20

① ② ③ ④ ⑤

20

① ② ③ ④ ⑤

20

① ② ③ ④ ⑤

20

① ② ③ ④ ⑤

"When you're eating, you should be eating—looking at the food, tasting the food in the atmosphere. I find that to be part and parcel to a good meal."

—DEBBIE HARRY

NOVEMBER
21

20

① ② ③ ④ ⑤

20

① ② ③ ④ ⑤

20

① ② ③ ④ ⑤

20

① ② ③ ④ ⑤

20

① ② ③ ④ ⑤

NOVEMBER
22

"There is no love sincerer than the love of food."

—GEORGE BERNARD SHAW

20

① ② ③ ④ ⑤

20

① ② ③ ④ ⑤

20

① ② ③ ④ ⑤

20

① ② ③ ④ ⑤

20

① ② ③ ④ ⑤

"You become a creative cook by first becoming a basic cook."
—JAMES BEARD

20

①
②
③
④
⑤

20

①
②
③
④
⑤

20

①
②
③
④
⑤

20

①
②
③
④
⑤

20

①
②
③
④
⑤

NOVEMBER
24

"The fridge broke, so I had to eat everything."

—JOEY TRIBBIANI, *FRIENDS*

20 ____

① ② ③ ④ ⑤

20 ____

① ② ③ ④ ⑤

20 ____

① ② ③ ④ ⑤

20 ____

① ② ③ ④ ⑤

20 ____

① ② ③ ④ ⑤

"A dish can lead two different chefs in two completely different directions. Everyone has their own style."

—DAVID WALTUCK

NOVEMBER
25

20 |
①
②
③
④
⑤

20 |
①
②
③
④
⑤

20 |
①
②
③
④
⑤

20 |
①
②
③
④
⑤

20 |
①
②
③
④
⑤

NOVEMBER
26

"As long as we can eat and write more books, that's really all I require."

—JOHN STEINBECK

20 _____

①
②
③
④
⑤

20 _____

①
②
③
④
⑤

20 _____

①
②
③
④
⑤

20 _____

①
②
③
④
⑤

20 _____

①
②
③
④
⑤

"I'd rather cook to satisfy a craving than cook for the intellect."
—TOM VALENTI

20

① ② ③ ④ ⑤

20

① ② ③ ④ ⑤

20

① ② ③ ④ ⑤

20

① ② ③ ④ ⑤

20

① ② ③ ④ ⑤

"One good dish, carefully prepared and eaten with pleasure, is an end—and a delight—in itself."

—DAVID TANIS

20

① ② ③ ④ ⑤

20

① ② ③ ④ ⑤

20

① ② ③ ④ ⑤

20

① ② ③ ④ ⑤

20

① ② ③ ④ ⑤

NOVEMBER
29

"I fell in love with French food—the tastes, the processes, the history, the endless variations, the rigorous discipline, the creativity, the wonderful people, the equipment, the rituals."
—JULIA CHILD

20

① ② ③ ④ ⑤

20

① ② ③ ④ ⑤

20

① ② ③ ④ ⑤

20

① ② ③ ④ ⑤

20

① ② ③ ④ ⑤

NOVEMBER

30

"The food I'm drawn to is the food that tells us who we are and what we are. It can have personality, heartache, and rebirth all on one plate. What better way to tell our story?"

—KELIS

20 ___

① ② ③ ④ ⑤

20 ___

① ② ③ ④ ⑤

20 ___

① ② ③ ④ ⑤

20 ___

① ② ③ ④ ⑤

20 ___

① ② ③ ④ ⑤

"Once you understand how a recipe works and why you're cooking it this way, that's what empowers you as a cook to be able to then go and adapt it."

—J. KENJI LOPEZ-ALT

20

① ② ③ ④ ⑤

20

① ② ③ ④ ⑤

20

① ② ③ ④ ⑤

20

① ② ③ ④ ⑤

20

① ② ③ ④ ⑤

"If more of us valued food and cheer and song above hoarded gold, it would be a merrier world."

—J.R.R. TOLKIEN, *THE HOBBIT*

20

① ② ③ ④ ⑤

20

① ② ③ ④ ⑤

20

① ② ③ ④ ⑤

20

① ② ③ ④ ⑤

20

① ② ③ ④ ⑤

> *"I think eating well is awfully important, why eat just to stay alive as most people do?"*
>
> —MARGARET ATWOOD, *THE EDIBLE WOMAN*

DECEMBER 3

20

①
②
③
④
⑤

20

①
②
③
④
⑤

20

①
②
③
④
⑤

20

①
②
③
④
⑤

20

①
②
③
④
⑤

DECEMBER

4

"My mother was a really good meal planner. The first thing she thought about after waking up and yelling at my father was, 'What will we be having for dinner?'"

—AMY SEDARIS

20 _____

① ② ③ ④ ⑤

20 _____

① ② ③ ④ ⑤

20 _____

① ② ③ ④ ⑤

20 _____

① ② ③ ④ ⑤

20 _____

① ② ③ ④ ⑤

"Strange to see how a good dinner and feasting reconciles everybody."

—SAMUEL PEPYS

20

①
②
③
④
⑤

20

①
②
③
④
⑤

20

①
②
③
④
⑤

20

①
②
③
④
⑤

20

①
②
③
④
⑤

"If you are ever at a loss to support a flagging conversation, introduce the subject of eating."

—LEIGH HUNT

20 ____

①
②
③
④
⑤

20 ____

①
②
③
④
⑤

20 ____

①
②
③
④
⑤

20 ____

①
②
③
④
⑤

20 ____

①
②
③
④
⑤

"When you are interested in la grande cuisine, you can't think of money, or you are licked from the start."

—FERNAND POINT

DECEMBER

7

20 ___

① ___
② ___
③ ___
④ ___
⑤ ___

20 ___

① ___
② ___
③ ___
④ ___
⑤ ___

20 ___

① ___
② ___
③ ___
④ ___
⑤ ___

20 ___

① ___
② ___
③ ___
④ ___
⑤ ___

20 ___

① ___
② ___
③ ___
④ ___
⑤ ___

DECEMBER 8

"Leave the gun. Take the cannoli."

—CLEMENZA, *THE GODFATHER*

20

① ② ③ ④ ⑤

20

① ② ③ ④ ⑤

20

① ② ③ ④ ⑤

20

① ② ③ ④ ⑤

20

① ② ③ ④ ⑤

"How easily happiness begins by /
dicing onions."

—WILLIAM MATTHEWS, "ONIONS"

9

20

①
②
③
④
⑤

20

①
②
③
④
⑤

20

①
②
③
④
⑤

20

①
②
③
④
⑤

20

①
②
③
④
⑤

"The primary requisite for writing well
about food is a good appetite."

—A.J. LIEBLING

20

① ② ③ ④ ⑤

20

① ② ③ ④ ⑤

20

① ② ③ ④ ⑤

20

① ② ③ ④ ⑤

20

① ② ③ ④ ⑤

"How can you create something significant unless you are happy when you do it?"

—BEN SHEWRY

DECEMBER
11

20 ___

①
②
③
④
⑤

20 ___

①
②
③
④
⑤

20 ___

①
②
③
④
⑤

20 ___

①
②
③
④
⑤

20 ___

①
②
③
④
⑤

"Thinking about spaghetti that boils eternally
but is never done is a sad, sad thing."
—HARUKI MURAKAMI, "THE YEAR OF SPAGHETTI"

20

① ② ③ ④ ⑤

20

① ② ③ ④ ⑤

20

① ② ③ ④ ⑤

20

① ② ③ ④ ⑤

20

① ② ③ ④ ⑤

"Our three basic needs, for food and security and love, are so mixed and mingled and entwined that we cannot straightly think of one without the others."

—M.F.K. FISHER

20 _____
① _____
_____
② _____
_____
③ _____
_____
④ _____
_____
⑤ _____

20 _____
① _____
_____
② _____
_____
③ _____
_____
④ _____
_____
⑤ _____

20 _____
① _____
_____
② _____
_____
③ _____
_____
④ _____
_____
⑤ _____

20 _____
① _____
_____
② _____
_____
③ _____
_____
④ _____
_____
⑤ _____

20 _____
① _____
_____
② _____
_____
③ _____
_____
④ _____
_____
⑤ _____

"We have found that there is nothing like a good lunch to give us an appetite for dinner."

—PETER MAYLE

20

① ② ③ ④ ⑤

20

① ② ③ ④ ⑤

20

① ② ③ ④ ⑤

20

① ② ③ ④ ⑤

20

① ② ③ ④ ⑤

"Food is the royal road to the unconscious."

—AMANDA HESSER

20

① ② ③ ④ ⑤

20

① ② ③ ④ ⑤

20

① ② ③ ④ ⑤

20

① ② ③ ④ ⑤

20

① ② ③ ④ ⑤

"Growing up I dreamed of garlic the way some dream of bright city lights."

—GARY SHTEYNGART

20 ___

① __
② __
③ __
④ __
⑤ __

20 ___

① __
② __
③ __
④ __
⑤ __

20 ___

① __
② __
③ __
④ __
⑤ __

20 ___

① __
② __
③ __
④ __
⑤ __

20 ___

① __
② __
③ __
④ __
⑤ __

*"More hands, less gadgets. The more I can use
my hands to make things, the better."*

—MARC VETRI

DECEMBER
17

20

① ② ③ ④ ⑤

20

① ② ③ ④ ⑤

20

① ② ③ ④ ⑤

20

① ② ③ ④ ⑤

20

① ② ③ ④ ⑤

*"We must have a pie. Stress cannot
exist in the presence of a pie."*
—DAVID MAMET, *BOSTON MARRIAGE*

20

① ② ③ ④ ⑤

20

① ② ③ ④ ⑤

20

① ② ③ ④ ⑤

20

① ② ③ ④ ⑤

20

① ② ③ ④ ⑤

"Love and eggs are best when they are fresh."

—ROBERTSON DAVIES

DECEMBER

19

20

① ② ③ ④ ⑤

20

① ② ③ ④ ⑤

20

① ② ③ ④ ⑤

20

① ② ③ ④ ⑤

20

① ② ③ ④ ⑤

"The slow ceremony of food kept them wordless and full of wonder."
—THOMAS LYNCH, *THE UNDERTAKING*

20 _____

①
②
③
④
⑤

20 _____

①
②
③
④
⑤

20 _____

①
②
③
④
⑤

20 _____

①
②
③
④
⑤

20 _____

①
②
③
④
⑤

"I discovered that no matter how much time you spent cooking dinner, when you fed people dessert, they were happiest."

—DORIE GREENSPAN

DECEMBER
21

20 _____

① ___
② ___
③ ___
④ ___
⑤ ___

20 _____

① ___
② ___
③ ___
④ ___
⑤ ___

20 _____

① ___
② ___
③ ___
④ ___
⑤ ___

20 _____

① ___
② ___
③ ___
④ ___
⑤ ___

20 _____

① ___
② ___
③ ___
④ ___
⑤ ___

"*I remember better what I've eaten than what I've thought.*"

—CHARLES SIMIC

20 _____

① ② ③ ④ ⑤

20 _____

① ② ③ ④ ⑤

20 _____

① ② ③ ④ ⑤

20 _____

① ② ③ ④ ⑤

20 _____

① ② ③ ④ ⑤

"Winter is my favorite season because of the food and the smells and the spices and how everyone is feeling everything so intensely.... It's the most perfect time for baking for people you love."

—TAYLOR SWIFT

DECEMBER

23

20 _____

_____
① ② ③ ④ ⑤

20 _____

_____
① ② ③ ④ ⑤

20 _____

_____
① ② ③ ④ ⑤

20 _____

_____
① ② ③ ④ ⑤

20 _____

_____
① ② ③ ④ ⑤

DECEMBER
24

"As you get more mature, you take all the superfluous things away and you get the essential flavor. Now I cook for people, not for myself."

—JEAN-GEORGES VONGERICHTEN

20 _____

① _____
② _____
③ _____
④ _____
⑤ _____

20 _____

① _____
② _____
③ _____
④ _____
⑤ _____

20 _____

① _____
② _____
③ _____
④ _____
⑤ _____

20 _____

① _____
② _____
③ _____
④ _____
⑤ _____

20 _____

① _____
② _____
③ _____
④ _____
⑤ _____

"Winter is the time for comfort, for good food and warmth, for the touch of a friendly hand and for a talk beside the fire: it is the time for home."

—EDITH SITWELL

20

①
②
③
④
⑤

20

①
②
③
④
⑤

20

①
②
③
④
⑤

20

①
②
③
④
⑤

20

①
②
③
④
⑤

DECEMBER
26

"Food is with the heart. Everything people do has to be done with passion. Cooking, music, architecture, politics—you can't do anything without passion."

—NOBUYUKI MATSUHISA

20 ___

① ②
③ ④ ⑤

20 ___

① ②
③ ④ ⑤

20 ___

① ②
③ ④ ⑤

20 ___

① ②
③ ④ ⑤

20 ___

① ②
③ ④ ⑤

"Good food is a lot like travel. It stimulates and surprises. It satisfies our craving for the exotic and the unknown. Good food is an adventure."

—ALFRED PORTALE

DECEMBER
27

20

① ② ③ ④ ⑤

20

① ② ③ ④ ⑤

20

① ② ③ ④ ⑤

20

① ② ③ ④ ⑤

20

① ② ③ ④ ⑤

DECEMBER
28

"When I sit down with a friend, no matter what I eat, it's good for me."

—CAMERON DIAZ

20

1
2
3
4
5

20

1
2
3
4
5

20

1
2
3
4
5

20

1
2
3
4
5

20

1
2
3
4
5

*"One cannot think well, love well, sleep
well, if one has not dined well."*

—VIRGINIA WOOLF

20

① ② ③ ④ ⑤

20

① ② ③ ④ ⑤

20

① ② ③ ④ ⑤

20

① ② ③ ④ ⑤

20

① ② ③ ④ ⑤

"The discovery of a new dish does more for human happiness than the discovery of a star."

—JEAN ANTHELME BRILLAT-SAVARIN

20

①
②
③
④
⑤

20

①
②
③
④
⑤

20

①
②
③
④
⑤

20

①
②
③
④
⑤

20

①
②
③
④
⑤

"At the end of the day it's food and you need to enjoy it. If it's a labor of love that you learn about every day, then you have figured out my secret: Food is a beautifully endless topic."

—HUGH ACHESON

DECEMBER
31

20 _____
_____ ①
_____ ②
_____ ③
_____ ④
                                          ⑤

20 _____
_____ ①
_____ ②
_____ ③
_____ ④
                                          ⑤

20 _____
_____ ①
_____ ②
_____ ③
_____ ④
                                          ⑤

20 _____
_____ ①
_____ ②
_____ ③
_____ ④
                                          ⑤

20 _____
_____ ①
_____ ②
_____ ③
_____ ④
                                          ⑤

Meals to Remember

DATE	THE DEAL WITH THE MEAL
.... / .... /	
.... / .... /	
.... / .... /	
.... / .... /	
.... / .... /	
.... / .... /	
.... / .... /	
.... / .... /	
.... / .... /	
.... / .... /	
.... / .... /	
.... / .... /	
.... / .... /	
.... / .... /	
.... / .... /	

Recipe Box

RECIPE NAME

FROM THE KITCHEN OF

SERVES

INGREDIENTS

DIRECTIONS

Recipe Box

RECIPE NAME

FROM THE KITCHEN OF

SERVES

INGREDIENTS

DIRECTIONS

Recipe Box

RECIPE NAME

FROM THE KITCHEN OF

SERVES

INGREDIENTS

DIRECTIONS

Recipe Box

RECIPE NAME

FROM THE KITCHEN OF

SERVES

INGREDIENTS

DIRECTIONS

Recipe Box

RECIPE NAME

FROM THE KITCHEN OF

SERVES

INGREDIENTS

DIRECTIONS

Recipe Box

RECIPE NAME

FROM THE KITCHEN OF   SERVES

INGREDIENTS

DIRECTIONS